D1232465

FRONT COVER

Bunsby Islands, near Kyuquot Sound on the northwest coast of Vancouver Island. This remote area protects and nourishes a new colony of sea otter, a major transplant from Amchitka Island in Alaska. Sea otter pelts led to the exploration of this coast by fur traders, and the hapless species was hunted almost to extinction. Here in this rugged sanctuary they are staging a strong comeback after almost a century's absence.

1

Chief Maquinna.

"*He did his work at summertime.*
He waxed strong; his possessions increased with his toil.
With the thunderdrum he sang at wintertime,
Great feasts he gave because his heart was full,
He sang of deeds and glories won by his house and his clan.
He was at peace with his God; his life indeed was full."

George Clutesi.

Captain George Vancouver, R.N.

"To describe the beauties of this region, will, on some future
occasion be a grateful task to the pen of a skillful panegyrist.
The serenity of the climate, the innumerable pleasing landscapes,
and the abundant fertility that nature puts forth, require only
to be enriched by the industry of man with villages, mansions,
cottages and other buildings, to render it the most lovely country
that can be imagined."

George Vancouver

4

Milestones on VANCOUVER ISLAND

historical & present day
attractions along
its roads and highways

by **Ken Pattison**

a
milestone publication

Copyright @ 1973
Kenneth M. Pattison

First printing August 1973
Revised edition May 1974
Third printing 1978
Fourth printing 1983
Revised edition May 1986

Published by
Pattison Ventures Ltd., 1572 Brodick Crescent,
Victoria, B.C., Canada V8N 1N4

Drawings, maps, layout and design by Jim Weston.
Typeset by Vancouver Freelance Litho-prep Limited
Printed and bound in Canada by Friesen Printers.

Canadian Cataloguing in Publication Data

Pattison, Ken, 1912-
Milestones On Vancouver Island

Includes index.
ISBN 0-919828-10-8
1. Vancouver Island, (B.C.) – Description
and travel – Guide-books. 2. Historic Sites –
Vancouver Island – Guide-books. 1. Title.
FC3844.2.P38   1986 917.11'34'044   C86-091115-2
F1089.V3P38   1986

FRONTISPIECE

The Comox Valley looking westward to Courtenay and the Comox Glacier within Strathcona Provincial Park. Eric J. Cooke photograph.

This book
is dedicated
to my wife Mary
and
Stephen
Alan
Maria
Laura
Eric

Beacon Hill Park.

Standing in Beacon Hill park, this totem pole (127'7'') is claimed to be the tallest in the world. A bronze plaque tells the story of the symbolic figures ornamenting its entire length.

An example of the excellent golf courses found on the Island.

S.S. Princess Marguerite leaving Victoria's harbour for Seattle.

Preface

Not many regions of North America have such varied scenic beauty as has British Columbia's Vancouver Island. Within its slightly less than 300 mile length, the visitor and resident alike can be treated to the wonders of total wilderness, or the delights of a modern sophisticated city.

It is but a short two hundred years since Captain Cook landed on the northwest coast of the Island and even less since the first small settlement began in Victoria. Nevertheless, in that short space of time, the Island has accumulated much of the history of human endeavour.

The melding of this history with modern attractions, placed in a natural environment of incomparable beauty, offers a theme hard to resist, be you writer or reader. Obviously Chess Lyons could not resist it when he wrote the first edition of Milestones On Vancouver Island in 1958.

In the fifteen years since then, much additional history has come to light, access to more areas is now possible and many new, recreational opportunities have been created. This new edition is, therefore a radical change from the original, providing the reader with a fresh look at this paradise, this Island.

How can I adequately thank my son Stephen for the number of times he read my material and said, "try another draft". Much of whatever quality there is, is because of his prodding. The research he helped with and the admirable way he put together the opening chapters will, I hope, result in thanks through the reader's enjoyment.

When I made a query about help with the general design an informant, without hesitation said, "get Jim Weston". His demanding standards and the quality of his own contributions of maps, illustrative material, choice of photographs and general layout design, have helped immeasurably in the reach for excellence.

Betty O'Neil read the manuscript and put verbs in where verbs were not, adding a word to my vocabulary – syntax.

The many provincial government departments: Archives, Museum, Parks, Highways, Forestry, Wildlife, Historical Sites and Travel Industry – the list seems endless – were a bountiful source of information and encouragement, for which I am grateful.

To family and friends, my heartfelt thanks for your patience and understanding, and to Chess Lyons for making it possible for me to indulge in this "labour of love".

K.M. Pattison

Victoria, British Columbia
June 1973

The re-opening of the Crystal Gardens at Victoria in the south and the building of the last link in the Island's main highway to Port Hardy in the north, are examples of the many changes that have occured since the last edition. Nearly all communities have created something new of interest to resident and visitor alike. A new museum in Sooke and additional skiing facilities up-island, are examples of the efforts that make our island a pleasant and exciting place to live in or visit.

But changes continue and while the information in this edition are as factual as possible, the reader should contact local sources for new, and additional interests.

K.M. Pattison

Victoria, British Columbia
March 1986

PIONEER NAVIGATORS

Before you lies one of the most intricate coastlines in the world. Into this sheltered strait, ageless domain of the Indian, sailed José Narváez in the year 1791. Other Spaniards and George Vancouver followed. Fighting wind and tide, they charted this remote maze of waterways — a milestone in the mapping of the world.

DEPARTMENT OF
RECREATION & CONSERVATION

This Stop-Of-Interest plaque overlooks the Strait of Georgia near the B.C. Ferry terminal at Horseshoe Bay, where travellers board ship for Vancouver Island. Similar plaques are found throughout the province, providing an opportunity to reflect on the people and events which have helped to mould our heritage.

Contents

Easter Lilies.

14

Milestone Guides

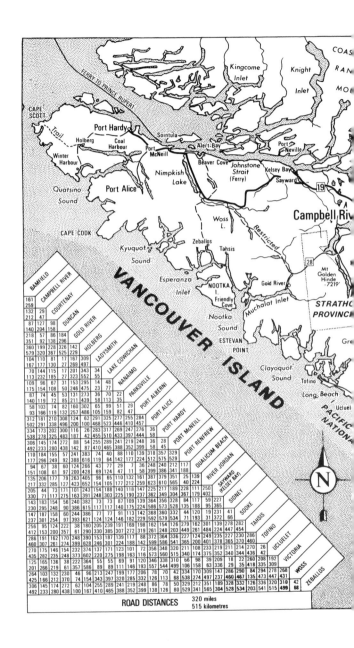

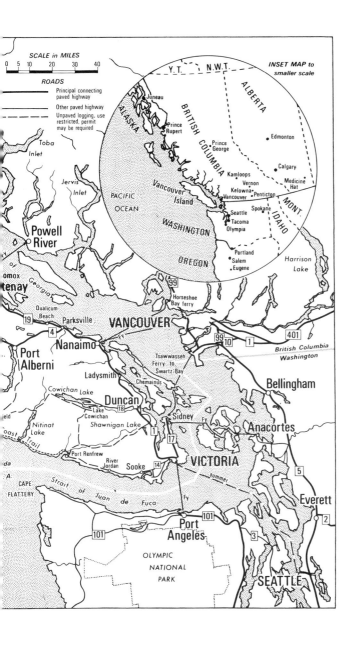

SCALE in MILES
0 5 10   20   30   40

ROADS

Principal connecting
paved highway

Other paved highway

Unpaved logging, use
restricted, permit
may be required

INSET MAP to
smaller scale

Y.T.   N.W.T.

ALBERTA

ALASKA

Juneau

BRITISH COLUMBIA

Prince Rupert

Prince George

Edmonton

Calgary

Kamloops

Vernon
Kelowna
Penticton
Vancouver

Medicine Hat

Vancouver Island

PACIFIC OCEAN

Seattle
Tacoma
Olympia

Spokane

WASHINGTON

MONT.

IDAHO

Portland
Salem
Eugene

OREGON

Harrison Lake

Toba Inlet

Jervis Inlet

Powell River

Georgia

Qualicum Beach

Parksville

99

Horseshoe Bay ferry

omox

tenay

19

4

VANCOUVER

99 10

1

401

Nanaimo

Fy

British Columbia
Washington

Port Alberni

Ladysmith

Chemainus

Tsawwassen
Ferry to
Swartz Bay

Bellingham

Cowichan Lake

Duncan

18

Lake Cowichan

Shawnigan Lake

Sidney

Fy

Anacortes

field

Nitinat Lake

oast Trail

Port Renfrew

River Jordan

1

17

VICTORIA

5

da

A.

CAPE FLATTERY

Sooke

14

summer

Everett

Strait

of

Juan

de

Fuca

Fy

2

101

Port Angeles

101

3

OLYMPIC

NATIONAL

PARK

SEATTLE

17

The flowering dogwood is the floral emblem of the province of British Columbia. The tree will grow from 10 to 30 feet high, bloom from April to June and sometimes again in September. It is protected by law against cutting.

18

This Island

OUT on the far northwestern coast of North America, where Canada's western mountains step into the Pacific, lies the very special land of Vancouver Island. It's very much an island of the sea, this young rugged land; here the mountains and the sea meet and contest each other, here they are seen at their finest.

Only an astronaut riding high and circling the globe could properly enjoy the Island's awesome panorama. Stretched out far below, it would be easily seen as North America's largest Pacific island, a massive 300 mile-long breakwater along the west coast. A maze of inlets and smaller islands break up the shoreline. Many narrow fiord-like inlets wind miles in from the open sea. The Island's interior is a fortress of mountains where long, still lakes lie in quiet fastness. It's a land of magnificent and dramatic proportions surrounded by the sea yet reaching for the skies, carpeted in deep green forests, and largely unfettered by settlement.

The Island exists because of its mountains: some of the shining snow-covered peaks reach over 6000 feet above sea level. Fully four-fifths of the Island is above 500 feet elevation. The Island's mountainous backbone is part of the Insular Mountain Range which dips northward below the sea, reappearing in the Queen Charlotte Islands. Vancouver Island, the largest and longest section of this young range, stands as the outpost of a continent, taking the brunt of storms spawned far out in the Pacific.

The sea always works to reclaim its own, however. Vancouver Island not only takes a regular lashing from Pacific weather, but once laboured under the groaning weight of accumulated weather – the great age of glaciers. During the recent "Ice Ages" the surface of Vancouver Island had quite a "scrubbing". Ponderous sheets of ice, some thousands of feet thick, slowly ground their way down out of the high mountains, scouring out valleys in their crushing drive to the sea. These "rivers of ice" carried away all topsoil and loose rock and left dramatically sculpted peaks and rock faces in their wake. Rocky debris, gravel beds, and silted terraces left by the melting ice can be seen almost everywhere on the Island.

DESIGN OF THE LAND

Vancouver Island's "physiography" – that is, its basic landform, is easily dominated by the Insular Mountain Range – but not entirely. Ribbons of lowland lie along the Island's east and west coasts, and large regions of low rolling hills lie at the northern and southern tips.

The Insular Mountains are the tips of massive granite batholiths which forced and buckled their way above sea level, taking great sections of sea bed up with them. They climax in height and complexity at the Island's centre, in Strathcona Park. Here the Golden Hinde (7,219 feet) lords over its close rivals in a mountain kingdom of lonely peaks and alpine glaciers. Summit elevations diminish from this point outwards along the mountain chain, with no peaks higher than 5,000 feet to be found northwest of Nimpkish Lake or southeast of Cowichan Lake.

Alberni Basin, also near the Island's centre, is a major exception to this mountainous pattern. The five to eight mile-wide Basin extends 25 miles northwestward beyond Port Alberni. Its low relief is dramatically offset by the abrupt valley wall on its eastern side, an old fault-line forming the western edge of the Beaufort mountain range.

Northern Vancouver Island subsides into the Nahwitti Lowland, whose low rounded hills seldom reach higher than 2,000 feet. Between Port McNeill and Port Hardy is the Sasquash

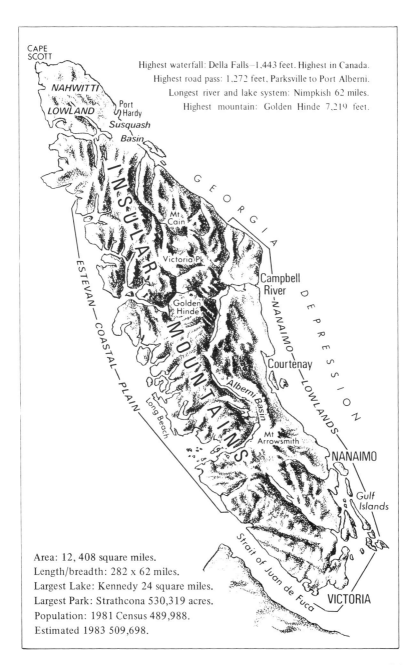

CAPE SCOTT

NAHWITTI LOWLAND

Port Hardy

Susquash Basin

INSULAR

GEORGIA

Mt. Cain

Victoria Pk.

ESTEVAN — COASTAL — PLAIN

Golden Hinde

MOUNTAINS

Campbell River

DEPRESSION

Courtenay

NANAIMO — LOWLANDS

Alberni Basin

Long Beach

Mt Arrowsmith

NANAIMO

Gulf Islands

Strait of Juan de Fuca

VICTORIA

Highest waterfall: Della Falls –1,443 feet. Highest in Canada.
Highest road pass: 1,272 feet, Parksville to Port Alberni.
Longest river and lake system: Nimpkish 62 miles.
Highest mountain: Golden Hinde 7,219 feet.

Area: 12, 408 square miles.
Length/breadth: 282 x 62 miles.
Largest Lake: Kennedy 24 square miles.
Largest Park: Strathcona 530,319 acres.
Population: 1981 Census 489,988.
Estimated 1983 509,698.

Basin, a lower basin of soft sedimentary rock under 1,000 feet elevation.

Along the west coast, the narrow Estevan Coastal Plain breaks the mountains' march into the sea. It's a one to two mile-wide lowland, frequently intersected by inlets. It extends almost 170 miles along the coast, seldom rising to heights above 150 feet. The Long Beach area is one of the major sections of this plain. Along the mountains' eastern flank and including the Gulf Islands, lie the Nanaimo Lowlands, a strip of low country running 175 miles from Sayward down the coast and past Victoria to Jordan River.

During periods of heavy glaciation rivers of ice flowed into the Strait of Georgia (the "Georgia Depression") from mountain valleys on both sides. Ice accumulated to depths of as much as 7,500 feet and depressed the land an additional 500 to 1,000 feet beneath its great weight. This massive iceflow spread southward and into the Strait of Juan de Fuca before it dissipated at sea.

Sedimentation from marine, glacial, and river sources interplayed continually as the ice ages warmed and the land rose, creating the low wooded terraces and narrow valleys seen along this coastline.

Progressively relieved of the burden of thousands of tons of ice, the Island is still slowly "bouncing" back, and has risen as much as 300 feet in places, creating various beach levels and terraces featured along the Island's east and north coasts. Owing to the tilt in the Island's rise, however, the west coast rose little. Instead the sea captured and flooded the coastal valleys as the glaciers retreated. Some of these "drowned valleys" reach deep into the Island's interior, almost severing it in several places. The longest, Alberni Inlet, has a depth of 1,125 feet and reaches inland over 40 miles.

CLIMATE AND VEGETATION

Vancouver Island, indeed the entire B.C. coast, lies in the path of the Japanese current, an ocean river of warm tropical water that circulates across the north Pacific and down the western coast of the continent. As it flows, the current releases its warmth in the form of banks of warm vapor which the prevailing westerly winds drive shoreward. The coastline is constantly warmed and often drenched as the moisture-laden air struggles to rise up over the mountains. There are no severe seasonal changes in this climate except for moderate temperature variations. Precipitation increases measureably in the cooler winter months, while the summer is remarkable for its low rainfall and sunny skies.

This moist but moderate weather nourishes a lush dense cloak of vegetation from tidewater to high alpine areas throughout the Island. On the western slopes and lowlands where incoming weather drops 60 to 100 inches of precipitation annually, and often more, the red and yellow cedars, hemlock, and balsam fir flourish in lush "rain forests". Higher, on better-drained mountain slopes and in protected valleys the giant Douglas fir and cedars mature to heights in excess of 200 feet, creating deep-shadowed forests. Often individual trees attain even greater heights, rivalling California's giant redwoods. Along the drier east coast, lying in the "rain shadow" of the mountains Douglas firs compete with maples, alder, dogwood, Garry oak, and arbutus trees. Rainfall continues to decrease and sunshine increases towards the south-east corner of the Island and the maze of Gulf Islands offshore. With less than 35 inches of precipitation annually and long hot summers, this area has an almost Mediterranean-style climate. Arbutus, Garry oaks, maples, spacious firs, and more open parkland vegetation dominate the landscape.

Most of the damper areas of the Island also support a thick undergrowth of plants that enjoy heavy moisture and shade; ferns, devil's club, mosses, salal, salmon berries, blueberries and other "brambles" and shrubs. In the drier southeast, the widespread and hardy broom actually an early "import" from Scotland, spread their bright yellow blossoms.

Man has done much in recent decades to alter the appearance of much of the Island. Agriculture, forestry, mining, and other resource developments coupled with roads and increasing settlement have fostered a growing human landscape, superimposed on the Island's natural landscape. Logging has removed the great primeval forests decades ago, agriculture led to the

A stand of virgin Douglas fir near the Nanaimo Lakes.

clearing of farms and ranches along the eastern and southern coasts, coal and copper mining led to extensive development in some areas, and now tourism, built on the "aesthetic" resources of an attractive land and climate, is ushering in further changes to the land.

AGRICULTURE

From its early beginnings around the colonial capital at Victoria, farming has spread up the Island's narrow eastern coast and some separate valleys, thriving on the rich lowlands of glacial till and river alluvium. It took patience and a lot of hard work by early pioneers to clear the heavy forests for planting, but now almost all the arable land is in some form of agricultural use. Several Scandinavian farming co-operatives valiantly tried to pioneer new farms farther up Island near Quatsino and Cape Scott, but limitations of climate, poor soil, and isolation combined to defeat them.

Hay and pasture for livestock, vegetables, dairying and poultry raising are the main agricultural operations. In the Saanich peninsula near Victoria, farmers also produce cut-flowers and bulbs, fruits, hothouse vegetables, and specialty crops. And on the Gulf Islands large sheep ranches have long been operating; some sheep have even gone wild. Most of the Island, however, being "vertical real estate", poor of soil, and heavily treed, is unsuitable for agriculture.

A lot of wholesome "farm-fresh" produce – vegetables, fruits, honey – is sold from roadside farm-stands along many country roads

FORESTRY

Timber was the first great resource to be harnessed to the energy, ingenuity, and voracity of modern industry. Great virgin forests were progressively felled and replaced with managed "tree farms" planted with selective high-yield species which are harvested well before maturity. Virgin or mature forests are now usually inaccessible or limited to parkland. Logging activity has fanned out into the interior valleys and up the mountain slopes, lacing them with railroads and truck roads and leaving a "patch-work" of re-growth. Today forestry is by far the Island's largest industry in terms of men employed, processing plants in operation, and lumber and products produced. Most of the back-country is managed by forestry companies who permit only limited public access because of heavily-loaded trucks and a concern for accidental fire.

From logging sites in the mountains, logs are trucked to the mills, or in some cases trucked or railroaded down to tidewater, where they are graded, sorted and assembled into booms or loaded on barges for towing to the mills. Sawmills and processing mills for plywood, pulp and paper and lumber are to be found at many of the major centres of the Island such as Victoria, Sooke, Lake Cowichan, Chemainus, Nanaimo, Port Alberni, Tahsis, Campbell River, Port Alice and Gold River. Major species cut are Douglas fir, hemlock, cedar and balsam.

The forest industry as a whole gives direct employment to many thousands and yields products to the value of many millions annually. In a sense, much of the island is one big "tree farm", so predominate is this industry and its attendant services. Much of the production is for export, primarily to the United States and Japan.

FISHERY

The waters around Vancouver Island are a spectacular habitat for fish that feed on the fresh nutrient-rich tides sweeping the off-shore banks and channels. Fish, plankton, mollusks, sponges, tiny sea plants and "forests" of kelp share an environment as rich and competitive as that on the land.

Whales feeding off-shore, the largest bounty from the sea, were the prize catch in earlier times for the Nootka Indian villages on the west coast. Villagers trapped and speared in-migrating schools of salmon and herring, as well as gathering oysters, clams, abalone, kelp, hunting halibut and seal, or, if one had rank and the right weapons, the behemoths of the seas — the whales. Because today's mechanized large-scale whaling has all but eliminated the leviathans from the ocean, Canada, belatedly, has banned whaling, and the last Island whaling station at Coal Harbour is now closed.

26

Part of the fishing fleet at Bamfield on the west coast of the Island.

Under close management, salmon and herring stocks have been increased from earlier depletions and support a large fishery. Most Island ports, and especially Indian communities, have small fishing fleets, but Sooke, Victoria, Bamfield, Tofino, Ucluelet, Sointula, Port Hardy, Alert Bay, and Campbell River are the busier centres for the industry.

Most "runs" of salmon occur between early summer and mid-fall. Coho and spring salmon are taken early by trollers trailing sets of baited lines over the off-shore banks or in the tide rips where the currents stir up feed. Gill and purse-seine nets take sockeye, pink, chum and coho salmon, and herring, as they migrate in schools to sheltered spawning areas.

Bottom fishing and trawling reaps halibut, cod, and flounder; there is also a large shellfish industry around the Island, for oysters, clams, and mussels, as well as trapping for shrimp and crabs. There are limited hauls of oolakan (the oil fish), smelt, abalone, and even special seaweeds. No wonder most Islanders delight in seafood cuisine. Many fish the mountain streams for trout and steelhead, prize delicacies for a hungry and skilled fisherman.

MINING

Valuable deposits and mineralization occur in only a few locations on the Island, nevertheless there is a moderately strong mining industry. Large amounts of coal were mined in the sedimentary basins around Nanaimo and Cumberland until these deposits were exhausted. Big Sicker Mountain near Duncan once yielded gold, copper, silver, lead and zinc. Glacial and sedimentary deposits yield abundant quantities of clay, sand, gravels, limestone, and shale at various locations.

The Island's first miners were Chinese labourers based at Nootka set to panning gold by their Spanish overlords in the early 1790s. Some "colour" was found at what is now Gold River. Leechtown, in the hills behind Sooke produced the Island's only gold rush, a minor short-lived bonanza. The Privateer mine at Zeballos reaped a fortune in gold in the 1930s before it too was exhausted.

Today's major mines are located near Buttle Lake (copper, zinc, silver) and a large copper-molybdenum mine west of Port Hardy at Rupert Inlet. Coal deposits near Nanaimo and Campbell River are currently being considered for their viability by mining interests.

There has been extensive testing for oil deposits on the continental shelf off-shore, but no development is yet foreseen for this industry, the economic and environmental considerations being quite formidable.

WILDLIFE

Wildlife has a major part to play in the total Island environment and as the focus for some recreation, notably photography, birdwatching, hunting, and nature study.

Whales, porpoises, killer whales (really porpoises), sea lions, and harbour seals are often seen cruising the off-shore waters. Headlands and channels offer spectacular views of these creatures during certain seasons.

Roosevelt elk are the monarchs of the forests, but their failing numbers and hidden retreats make them less visible. Black-tailed deer, black bear, wolves, and the stealthy cougar

28

(mountain lion) also dwell in the forest sanctuaries. The concentration of cougar is reputed to be the greatest anywhere, but the wary and nocturnal habits of the cats and their dislike for human activity make them difficult to observe. They have retreated into the less-frequented portions of the mountains. Deer are the most frequently seen, usually feeding in open areas or in the succulent regrowth of logged areas.

Upland game birds are numerous, including grouse, pheasant, quail, and migratory wildfowl like the Canada and Snow Goose.

Curiously many animals never returned to the Island after the recent glaciation. Many common animals found on the mainland are not seen on the Island: grizzly bear, mountain goat, porcupine, skunk, coyote, and bobcat. Other Island species were directly "imported" including the pheasants, quail, foxes, chipmunks, muskrats and rabbits. A mountain goat transplant near Lake Cowichan a number of years ago has apparently failed, but recent transplants of sea otter from the doomed island of Amchitka in Alaska have hopefully "taken" on a lonely remote section of coast near the Island's northwest tip. See front cover

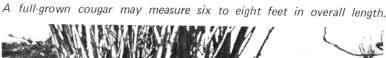

A full-grown cougar may measure six to eight feet in overall length.

photograph. It is hoped these amusing and attractive animals will eventually spread, under close protection, all along the coastline.

One of the most fascinating "transplants" has been that of the English skylark. In the early 1900s, well over a hundred pairs were released near Victoria and by 1962 it was estimated that 1000 of them inhabited various areas of the southern Island. Its lovely song and sustained warble continues as the bird soars to great heights. It then descends to earth in a series of swooping dives.

RECREATION

Probably the Island's fastest growing industry, recreation is amply encouraged by the great bounties of open space, wilderness, and the surrounding sea. Boating, fishing, swimming, beachcombing and other water-orientated activities occur all around the Island's shores and around mountain lakes and rivers. Hiking, mountaineering, skiing, hunting, bicycling and photography are increasingly attracting people to the outdoors, encouraged by increasing recreational access to whole sections of the Island.

Salmon fishing is possibly the most popular outdoor sport; the prized salmon runs are concentrated from April through October. Mountain streams and lakes yield cutthroat and rainbow trout, steelhead, Kokanee, and recently introduced Eastern brook trout. Boating and sailing are also tremendously popular, whether together with fishing or just for cruising the intricate coastline and off-shore islands. Island marinas are well-stocked with a variety of boats and services.

More than 50 provincial parks and a large national park serve recreational needs as well as preserving some of the original natural habitats. Strathcona is the largest park and straddles the Island's heartland; Pacific Rim National Park faces the open Pacific on the west; MacMillan Park husbands a "Cathedral Grove" of virgin forest, while whole islands off-shore are preserved as complete parks. Some are close to highways for maximum use by travellers, others are tucked away for future development, preserved as nature conservancies, or located for the specific needs of marine travellers.

30

Many parks feature government campsites and picnic spots with camping spaces, water, fuel, and nearby hiking trails. In addition there are many private facilities: campgrounds, motels, hotels, marinas, and resorts that serve the public, especially in the older built-up areas.

Montague Harbour on Galiano Island, one of the Gulf Island group adjacent to Vancouver Island

Friendly Cove in Nootka Sound, where Chief Maquinna and the Moachat band of Nootka had their summer village, Yuquot. This was the first native settlement seen by Europeans in what is now British Columbia. Cook, his officers and midshipman came in by ship's boats from their anchorage at Resolution Cove in April 1778. A cairn was erected on the site to commemorate the event.

Discovery and Colonization

THE far western coast of North America was a mystery to cartographers and explorers long after the settlement of the Atlantic coast of the "New World". What is now British Columbia received scant attention from Spanish, Russian, and British explorers, and it was not until the publishing of Captain Cook's journals that Europeans and Americans alike gained any idea of the size and appearance of this unknown corner of the Pacific. Britain's Captain Cook was apparently the first European explorer to go ashore in the region. In 1778 his party arrived at Nootka on the northwest coast of Vancouver Island. There they repaired and re-masted their ship, established trading contact with the natives, and surveyed and charted the surrounding waters. His exploits were later the basis of Britain's formal claim to the region in the face of the expansion of Spanish and Russian territories from the south and north respectively.

Captain Cook found the land attractive, if harsh, settled by hardy and resourceful natives, and rich in furs, fish, and timber. The soft dense sea otter furs were particularly appealing; the samples Cook's men took to the Orient and Europe caused widespread interest. For several decades thereafter furs were the basis of all further activity in the region. Navigators like Barkley, Vancouver, Narvaez, and Quimper extended chartwork, naming headlands and channels, while fur merchants, often the ambitious "Boston Traders", sought the prized sea otter furs from scattered coastal Indian villages.

Vancouver Island was established as an island by Captain Vancouver when he explored and charted Johnson Strait in 1792. He originally named his new-found island "Quadra and Vancouver's Island" to honour the commander of the Spanish fleet, who co-operated with him in the final settlement of the "Nootka Controversy." But the eclipse of the Spanish empire in the region, and common usage, reduced the name to its present form. However many of the Spanish and British place names on today's charts stem from this period of joint exploration.

Eventually the maritime furtraders were joined by the great fur companies from overland—the Nor'westers and the Hudson's Bay Company. Their empires were extended overland by Company traders who explored routes through the Rockies and down the torturous river canyons to the Pacific. In rapid succession Mackenzie reached Bella Coola (1793), Simon Fraser explored the river that bears his name (1808), and Thompson surveyed the Columbia to the sea at Astoria (1811).

THE COLUMBIA TERRITORY

Strong competition for trading privileges arose, complicated by the presence of Russian and American traders. However, through purchase, amalgamation, and skillful politics, the Hudson's Bay Company finally came to dominate the fur trade and establish control over the entire "Columbia" territory including Vancouver Island. This firmly implanted British economic and diplomatic roots on the Island, and paved the way for the development of colonial status and eventual union with the rest of "British" North America in the confederacy of Canada.

From their headquarters on the Columbia River, first at Fort George (Astoria) and later upriver at Fort Vancouver, the Hudson's Bay Company came to control a vast rich fur empire, stretching to Russian Alaska on the north, Spanish California in the south, and from the Rockies to the Sandwich Islands (Hawaii). A series of small forts in the interior served the inland travel routes, while most coastal trading was conducted from sailing vessels and the famous steamer "Beaver". The distinctive side-paddles and smoking stack of the Beaver made her a colourful "flagship" for the Company as she steamed into scattered Indian villages along the coast.

However, the Company was reluctant to encourage any colonization attempts involving settlers. They expected this activity would disturb the trade in furs, as it had repeatedly across Canada. Instead they viewed Columbia, and New Caledonia to the north, as a private preserve. Only one major development, an agricultural colony near Fort Vancouver, was encouraged, expressly to supply food, material, and men to the main post there. But the rest of the territory slumbered, distant, unknown, deep in the folds of the Company.

SETTLEMENT ON VANCOUVER ISLAND

Finally the pressure of world events, and westward march of settlement awoke the west coast to its continental future. Russian, British, and American governments sought stronger footholds on the coast, while land-hungry families struck out for the "Oregon Trail". The Hudson's Bay Company wisely decided to seek a more northerly headquarters free of pressure from incoming American settlers. Their growing numbers had already raised the question of Oregon's political future. Company headquarters could only be safe within British territory.

In 1842 a promising site at Camosack, on the southern tip of Vancouver Island, was surveyed for a new fort. "The place itself appears a perfect Eden in the midst of the dreary wilderness of the northwest coast," wrote chief factor James Douglas. The Company decided to move to "Eden" and Victoria became the first permanent European settlement on Vancouver Island and a headquarters for the fur business. And what more fitting a name than that of the great British Queen herself, sovereign over a vast and powerful world empire.

Victoria firmly established British presence on the northwest coast but the rest of the territory was swept into American hands. Under the Oregon Treaty in 1846, the 49th parallel was extended unbending clear across the mountains to the Pacific as the official border. Fort Vancouver on the Columbia River was left deep within American territory. Victoria fell heir to the mantle of territorial headquarters and was the focus of Pacific

35

politics and development until nearly the end of the century.

With the new boundary settled, the Foreign Office in London was forced to consider the problem of colonizing and retaining this remote portion of the realm. The growing tide of American settlers just below the border would continue to pose a threat to British dominance in this empty region. So Vancouver Island was made a Crown colony in 1849, to be administered by the Hudson's Bay Company with direct instructions to encourage settlement and strengthen the colony's future. But advertisements in Europe and Canada failed to excite wide interest; the new colony grew slowly and quietly and remained centred around the fort at Victoria.

Some modest development did emerge slowly. Under the auspices of the Puget Sound Agricultural Company, a subsidiary of the Hudson's Bay Company, groups of British settlers were brought to Victoria. They and their families opened up the lands around the new fort and helped the colony take root. Craigflower, Colwood, Uplands, and Lakewood were all large "Company farms" that provided some staples and produce. Many of the men also worked part-time for the Company on construction and road-building. Many local and up-island Indians also took interest in the proceedings; often they stayed to work on construction or on road gangs that laid paths to the outlying farms at Sooke and Saanichton. Small trades and services, lumbering, fishing, various crafts and the growing farms gradually expanded the little capital and fur centre. Victoria's warm climate and picturesque setting somewhat offset its location. Many Company pensioners, notably a colourful band of robust Canadien canoemen, joined the settlers. Esquimalt harbour, next to Victoria, became a major port-of-call for the British Pacific Fleet, expanding the military function of the new capital.

COAL AND NANAIMO

Rich seams of coal were discovered up-island by the shores of the Strait of Georgia. An earlier coal strike at Fort Rupert, near the north tip of the Island, having proved unprofitable, showed the new site as a more promising field; so in 1854 a new "Company town" was founded, with twenty-three miners and

36

Number 1 Shaft of the Vancouver Coal Company at Nanaimo had ten miles of tunneling, much of it under the sea bed. These workings were a pioneer effort in Canadian undersea mining, and no other mine had workings so far out under the sea.

their families brought out from Scotland to work the colleries.

In spite of its isolation from the capital, the new village of Colville, later renamed Nanaimo, set down sturdy roots ensuring its success. Nanaimo not only nurtured the coal business, but also lumbering, farming, and fishing. Nearby salt pans supplied commercial salt. And always there was the brisk trade in furs. In time, Nanaimo's growth encouraged fringe settlements at Cowichan, Chemainus, and Comox. Coal was to become synonomous with Nanaimo district for nearly a century.

GOLD RUSH DAYS

When stories arose of promising gold strikes on the Thompson and Fraser river banks, gold fever startled the coast. The gold rush might be officially recognized as starting in Victoria on Sunday, April 25, 1858. With electrifying effect, 450 gold-struck miners arrived aboard the side-wheeler "S.S. Commodore" and disembarked bag and baggage into the quiet village, anxious to voyage on to the goldfields. Victoria's astounded population was almost doubled. Within weeks other vessels disgorged additional hundreds and reported full bookings for future voyages. Most of the early miners were from the exhausted mines of California's '49 gold rush; others arrived from eastern Canada, the United States, Europe, and even China. Victoria, as the only port of entry and source of supplies for the entire region, became the focus for the gold rush. Most immigrants were would-be miners destined for the Fraser River; they paused in Victoria only long enough to arrange permits, supplies, and transport to the mainland. There they teemed over the gold-flecked bars and river banks, panning for "colour".

Fort Victoria's bastion, built in 1843.

Later the same year, November 1858, a new colony was proclaimed on the mainland to handle the political and administrative pressures of this unique migration. Vancouver Island's Governor, James Douglas, was also put in charge of this new colony, British Columbia, with a make-shift capital at small Fort Langley on the Fraser River. Douglas often visited among the miners, and found that "the general feeling is in favour of English rule on Fraser's River, the people having a degree of confidence in the sterling uprightness and integrity of Englishmen which they do not entertain for their own countrymen." Nevertheless, the presence of so many restless Americans was good reason to administer quickly and wisely.

Victoria quickly surged with growth and investment, transformed by the magic of gold from "merely a fur traders' colony clustered around Fort Victoria" to a burgeoning city. In 1862 Victoria was incorporated as western Canada's first city. It became a classical "boom town"—tents sprang up everywhere, followed by stores, warehouses, banks, shops, breweries, wharves, billiard halls, hotels, and many, many saloons. Often these businesses were financed by businessmen and speculators who followed the miners up from San Francisco.

An early view of Victoria: Yates Street looking east from Wharf Street.

The British Royal Navy's "Flying Squadron" in Esquimalt Harbour, 1869-70. Visits such as these contributed much to the social and economic life of the young and growing colony.

Victoria's first newspaper, the Victoria Gazette, published in June 1858, was produced by Americans from San Francisco, who joined the colonial business community following on the heels of the gold rush. This first paper was followed almost immediately by the Vancouver Island Gazette and a French language paper, Le Courrier de la Nouvelle Caledonie. Finally in December of that year the British Colonist came out, produced by a Nova Scotian, William Alexander Smith, who had changed his name to Amor de Cosmos. This was quite a boom in new newspapers for the formerly quiet colony, for previous news had been printed in San Francisco or brought in mail packets around Cape Horn.

The British Colonist survived many rivals and tribulations, its editor/publisher rising to become one of the political leaders of the new province. The Colonist, as it soon became known, and the Daily Times founded in 1884, became the Times-Colonist in 1980, spanning over a century of western Pacific history.

Land speculation soared as the city swelled. A town plan was developed, parks were set aside, farming and lumbering expanded, institutions were founded, and the harbour was declared a free port. The celebrated "bride-ships", "Tynemouth" and "Robert Lowe" brought badly needed brides and precipitated new families settling into the colony.

From the start the new colony had a British demeanor: most colonial officials, company men, and the militia were British, as were the first settlers and businessmen. Britons were active in commerce, the church, law, military and political affairs, and business management. Popular celebration of British holidays, sports, fraternal organizations, politics, architecture, social life, and even farming all strongly reflected ties with Britain.

The boom subsided in less than a decade as the gold fields became exhausted. But Victoria survived, its future assured. Now a far larger city, with a diverse economic base, the capital expanded its military and political roles. Britain's Pacific fleet spent greater periods at nearby Esquimalt. The mainland and island colonies united in 1866 with Victoria, except for a brief period, the capital over a vast new British Columbia.

Nanaimo missed the excitement and instability of being a gold rush boom town. But the town grew steadily, with increasing demands for coal, timber, and land for new farms. Elsewhere on Vancouver Island tentative new settlements arose—Cowichan, Chemainus, Alberni, Comox, Saanich, and Sooke. Instead of having bawdy miners and speculators to deal with, these outposts were occupied with the strenuous task of carving farms out of the heavy forests, building homes and barns, opening roads, and maintaining friendly relations with neighbouring Indian villages. Hardship and isolation took their toll, however, and growth in these remote settlements was slow.

Sealing fleet at rest in Victoria's Harbour in 1890. The bridge in the background is now the road and causeway in front of the Empress Hotel.

CONFEDERATION AND THE RAILROAD

After the gold rush the colony settled into a period of recession. The extravagance and growth nurtured by easy gold was over. The Hudson's Bay Company lost its fur monopoly, and increasing settlement made serious inroads on the Company's business. Recent American annexations of California and Oregon, and the purchase of Alaska in 1858, plus the presence of many American immigrants in the small colony, led to speculation on the possible triumph of "Manifest Destiny" and union with the United States. Others saw greater potential in union with Canada and a maintenance of "Loyalist" ties with the Crown.

42

Controversy raged until 1871 when the new colony of British Columbia joined the Canadian Confederation, enticed partly by the promise of a transcontinental rail link with the east. The railway was to be their champion; it would provide cheaper access to eastern markets, encourage employment, and bring settlers west. Yet railroad building did not begin until the 1880s and its eventual destination was Vancouver, not Victoria. In the interim decades, however, Victoria grew as the economic heart and capital of the new province. A great fleet of sealing schooners and fishing boats roamed out of Island ports; giant virgin timbered forests found their way into world lumber markets; pockets of farming grew in Island valleys, and the coal seams at Nanaimo seemed an inexhaustible bonanza.

The question of the route for the proposed railway to the Pacific became a sensitive and crucial issue with Victoria and other Island communities. Realizing their geographic handicap as an island, they urged that railroad planners and politicians consider the Homathko River route to the coast at Bute Inlet, where a series of bridges could span the narrow channels to Vancouver Island. To spur adoption of this route they proposed a railroad connecting Victoria and Nanaimo. The "Esquimalt and Nanaimo Railway" would move coal and timber shipments to port, and a short extension north of Nanaimo could meet the proposed transcontinental line. The "E & N Railway" was finally built in 1886 but it never met the main line. Instead, Port Moody by Burrard Inlet, (and shortly after, Vancouver) was selected as the Pacific terminus.

Losing a place on the trans-continental line was a bitter loss to Island residents, particularly since they helped negotiate for it when entering Confederation. The railroad's completion had a drastic unsettling effect on Island commerce and Victoria's supremacy as a trans-Pacific shipment point and economic centre of the province. The pace of Island resource development, settlement, and industry all began to fall behind the mainland growth.

Not until the Panama Canal was opened in 1914 did Victoria and other Island ports regain some of their past stature. Lumber and coal shipments in particular could take advantage of the new shorter water route to eastern markets. But by then Vancouver was well established as a major world port, railhead, and mercantile capital of the province.

Victoria was destined to remain basically a provincial capital, naval base and centre of Island commerce. Other Island communities slowly realized their potentials, usually manning agriculture and resource industries that led the Island's economic growth into the 20th Century.

THE SINEWS OF SETTLEMENT

The continued history of Vancouver Island is the story of overcoming the Island's physical barriers—linking isolated farming and logging settlements, urging new railroads through the mountains and into the timber-rich forests, developing rapid transport to the mainland, and serving the increasing demands of the automobile. When the population was small and scattered along the coast, steamers originally provided the only dependable means of communication and transport for goods. Coal mining and logging ushered in the age of railroads, greatly increasing the pace of Island development. Finally the private car and heavy trucks brought vast improvements in access roads and the construction of new faster highways linking communities and industrial sites. And the light float-plane has found increasing use into the smaller fishing ports and logging camps still isolated beyond the Island's highway system.

SHIPPING

Early fur traders arrived on the coast by sailing ships, trading from off their decks as they followed tides and weather round the intricate coastline. In 1836 the Hudson's Bay Company brought the first steamer to the region, the 100 foot side-paddler "Beaver". Powered by two 35 HP steam engines, the 109 ton vessel became the Company flagship and workhorse, continually active along the coast trading, surveying, and ferrying supplies to scattered settlements. She was finally wrecked at the entrance to Burrard Inlet in 1888 after a long and famous career.

Other H.B.C. ships were also operating around Vancouver Island in these early years. The barque "Columbia" of 310 tons sailed from England with the "Beaver" and was employed as the annual supply link with England. Other steamers such as the "Labouchere" and the "Otter" arrived and expanded trade and transport routes, followed in turn by the "Robert Dunsmuir", and the stern-wheelers "Western Slope", "Cariboo Fly", and the "Maude".

Rapid developments in logging, coal mining, and increased settlement and farming on the Island led to a number of shipping companies becoming active in connecting the scattered communities along the Island's coasts. The Union Steamship Co. was founded in 1889 and provided vital regular visits to Island points, often under very primitive conditions. Typical was the plight of the first settlers near Campbell River who had to row out into Discovery Passage to attract passing steamers. After a wharf was built, in 1906, and regular scheduled stops could be made, "boat days" became a regular social event of the week for these remote farmers and loggers.

The Canadian Pacific Railway entered the coast steamship business with the purchase of a small shipping company. They inaugurated the "triangle run" between Vancouver, Victoria, and Seattle in 1909 with the "Princess of Victoria". Other Princess "pocket liners" were built such as "Charlotte", "Kathleen", and the famous "Maquinna". The "Princess Maquinna" was built in Victoria in 1912 and became a favourite of loggers and fishermen along the Island's west coast. For almost forty

The S.S. "Princess Maquinna".

years she was often the sole connecting link with the outside world for many remote settlements with such interesting names as Kyuquot, Ahousat, Quatsino, Uchucklesit, Clo-oose, and Bamfield.

Increasing automobile traffic led the CPR to build the "Motor Princess" in 1923, a forty-car ferry which presaged a new era of car ferries. Eventually the CPR gave up the car ferry service, replaced by the modern system now provided by the very efficient B.C. Ferry Corporation.

Ships of the Northland Navigation Company and the Black Ball Line also served Vancouver Island points, the former around the exposed west coast and the latter on ferry and freight service to the mainland. However, their links and service to the Island no longer exist.

Today two smaller ships still provide transportation and communication to a number of settlements on the west coast. Barkley Sound has a daily service from Port Alberni to Ucluelet with the "M.V. Lady Rose". To the north, Nootka Sound Service operates a year round service with the 136 foot "M.V. Uchuck III" out of Gold River. Both the "Lady Rose" and the "Uchuck III" make special excursions during the summer months; the former to Bamfield and Ucluelet, and the latter to historic Friendly Cove in Nootka Sound.

Ferry connections between Vancouver Island and the mainland were formerly in the hands of private enterprise, but a seamen's strike in 1958 left the Island virtually isolated except for air transport. The strike was settled but the provincial government was determined that the main transportation link to the mainland would not be cut in future.

Swartz Bay at the tip of the Saanich peninsula, and Tsawwassen by the Fraser River delta, were selected as terminals for a new government service between the Island and the mainland. This was shortly followed by another route for central-Island service—from Departure Bay near Nanaimo to Horseshoe Bay in West Vancouver. The 342 foot "Queen of Victoria" launched in 1962 became the flagship and prototype for the major ferries in this fleet; she has five similar sister ships, the Queens of "Vancouver", "Esquimalt", "Saanich", "Burnaby", and "New Westminster". All these ships have undergone an interesting and innovative metamorphosis since their launching. First, upper car decks or ramps were built into the hold to increase vehicular capacity. Later each ship was in turn "stretched" from 342 feet to 426 feet by literally cutting apart the vessel amidships and adding a new 84 foot middle section. Now longer, with added decks and expanded passenger facilities, these six great "Queens" now transport about 200 cars plus hundreds of passengers on each trip speeding them at 18 knots across the waters to and from the Island.

The Ferry Authority and the Department of Highways have added or improved ferry routes connecting many of the smaller offshore islands. A new run was extended across the top of the Strait of Georgia from Comox to Powell River and regular service provided by B.C. Ferries from Port Hardy north to Prince

Rupert on the northern mainland, a 330 mile, 15 hour journey through the scenic "inside passage". This is the route taken by the many cruise ships running to Alaska.

Two American ferry lines also serve Vancouver Island connecting it with Washington State. A daily service from Anacortes through the San Juan Islands (the American "Gulf Islands") to Sidney is maintained by the Washington State Ferry authority. The Black Ball Line links Victoria with Port Angeles across the Strait of Juan de Fuca with the ferry "Coho".

RAILROADS

Vancouver Island's first railroad was built in anticipation of a link-up with the westward moving Canadian Pacific Railroad. The Esquimalt and Nanaimo Railroad was built by Island coal baron Robert Dunsmuir at a cost of $750,000. The Canadian Prime Minister John A. Macdonald drove the proverbial last spike at Shawnigan in 1886. However, the CPR wisely terminated at Vancouver, and the E. & N. R. R. had to seek its own destiny.

Gradually railroads expanded with the development of coal and logging, and the spread of settlement. Passenger and freight service provided a welcome alternative to the uncertainties of steamers and the difficulties of the overland roads and trails. The railway also reduced the cost of bringing timber to coast mills and agriculture produce to markets . . . making these enterprises more competitive.

In 1906 the E. & N. was purchased by the CPR and extended beyond Nanaimo. In 1911 the tracks reached across the Island to Port Alberni, and other extensions were placed into Lake Cowichan and to Courtenay.

By 1917 no less than two railroads and one electric interurban line served the length of the Saanich peninsula.

Separate logging railroads proliferated around the Island between 1915 and 1950. It has been estimated that for every mile of public railroad on the Island there was some thirty miles of logging railroad. However the logging railroads, like the larger

E and N Railway's passenger train pulling into the Strathcona Hotel at Shawnigan Lake at the turn of the century.

public railroads, felt increasing pressure from improvements in road construction and transport trucks. Most are now long gone, and the forests to this day remain laced with a web of old railway operations, in most cases a line of ties and rotting timber tressles in the bush. Only a few logging railroads remain, such as the Canadian Forest Product's Nimpkish line, perhaps the largest on the continent, that transports car-loads of timber down its 75 mile mainline to tidewater at Beaver Cove.

The great age of Island railroads is now largely a memory, preserved in the form of old steam locomotives on display at various Island points. The Forest Museum north of Duncan has an exciting train ride, and daily passenger service is still in effect over the CPR's E.&N. line from Victoria to Courtenay, a journey that can be made in one day.

ROADS

With the beginning of farming around Victoria, wagon roads were rough but essential supply and communication links. In 1851 a road to Sooke via Esquimalt and Metchosin was begun, and ten years later a rough trail was extended to Cowichan Bay. During the 1880's a rough coastal wagon road was pushed through from Victoria to Nanaimo. It was extended in 1886 to

Parksville, and, in the same year, the trail from Nanaimo to Alberni was widened into a wagon road.

The advent of the automobile forced the government to improve the Island's road system. The difficult Malahat route north of Victoria, rising to an elevation of 1,200 feet above Saanich Inlet, was finally completed in 1911. It took some courage and persistance to make the trip by car, and those that successfully travelled the route felt they had achieved a real feat. During the 20s and 30s there was little new construction of roads, although the Island highway was extended north beyond Campbell River to Kelsey Bay in the late 40s.

Real progress on modern roads has taken place over the past two decades. For example the Malahat was virtually reconstructed at a cost of $7,900,000. A new paved road was built from Campbell River to the "instant town" of Gold River on the west coast and work is now complete on the final link in the Island's main highway north to Port Hardy. A hard surface road from Port Alberni replaces former private logging roads, giving dependable access to Tofino, Ucluelet and the exciting Pacific Rim National Park on the west coast of the Island. Another west coast village, Port Renfrew, has now been linked to the Island highway system, formerly these areas had only limited access through rough and dangerous private industrial roads.

Like the logging railways of a previous era, a web of logging access roads has also been built through the forested interior. More and more of these logging roads have now been opened to public use on a restricted-time basis; gradually some are being transferred to the Department of Highways. Others have been improved and opened for regular public travel on weekends and holidays—such as the 100 mile industrial road from Gold River to Beaver Cove. During working hours, however, these roads are quite unsafe as heavy-laden radio-controlled logging trucks "barrel" down to dumping sites and back for fresh loads.

Although more roads will be built in the future, particularly in the Island's northern regions, the geography of the land makes construction costs very high. Also, the growing public concern for the preservation of unspoiled areas will act as a check on unlimited road construction.

AIR TRAVEL

The airplane, first flown on the Island in 1911, has opened up the remote coastal communities and mountain-bound logging camp, and vastly improved communications between scattered Island communities. The first scheduled flights between Victoria and Vancouver started in 1933.

During the Second World War, the Royal Canadian Air Force constructed the Patricia Bay airport and other wartime facilities on the Island. Many of these military airports later became civilian facilities. Victoria International Airport, located on the Saanich Peninsula, is the Island's main airport. Operated by Transport Canada, it provides through various carriers, service to the mainland and beyond. Other commercial airports serve the various Island centres. An excellent "harbour to harbour" service operates between Victoria and Vancouver.

Comox airport is part of the Canadian Armed Forces airbase "Comox" from which reconnaisance jets and patrol aircraft range the Canadian Pacific coast and where special search and rescue craft await distress calls from anywhere in the province.

From the discovery of Vancouver Island to the present, transportation has been a key factor in its development. Without the ships, railways, roads, and aircraft this rugged Island never could have been so extensively settled nor its economy developed to its present state.

The Empress forms a backdrop to the popular Tally-Ho and Victoria's famous hanging flower baskets.

Victoria

... a capital with style

THE gentle open glades, snug harbour, and easy access to the Strait of Georgia or the open Pacific made Camosack an ideal location for the new northern headquarters and military fort of the Hudson's Bay Company. James Douglas, the Company's chief factor, investigated the site in 1842 and concluded that "there was no sea-port north of the Columbia where so many advantages could be found combined. The place itself appears a perfect Eden in the midst of the dreary wilderness of the north west coast." The following year he ordered construction of the new fort.

Fort Victoria became the first European settlement on Vancouver Island and the new Company headquarters for all of what became known as "British Columbia". The new post, with its small band of Company men, British settlers, and neighbouring Indians was to emerge as the powerful, wealthy, and handsome capital of a vast province.

Victoria became home port for coastal trading vessels, great mercantile clipper-ships, and fishing and sealing fleets; neighbouring Esquimalt became the Pacific base for the powerful British Royal Navy. Victoria in the 19th Century grew to become the financial centre and capital for a bounteous and vast hinterland, and the largest port city north of San Francisco.

After completion of the Canadian Pacific Railroad in 1886, the new railhead city of Vancouver quickly began to usurp Victoria's prominence in shipping, commerce, finance, and distribution for the entire province. Victoria reluctantly "retired" to her roles as the seat of government, naval base, and the focus for a rich island fiefdom.

Now Victoria is content with being one of the more attractive and unique capital cities in Canada. From its frontier roots and "Empire" heritage the city has emerged a living archive, the repository of colonial history and architecture, a city of great fortunes and eminent citizens; the province's oldest and proudest city, still in the centre of political and military activity, a capital with style.

A LITTLE BIT OF ENGLAND

Victoria was tutored to become a shining jewel in Britain's far-flung empire; cricket in the park, fashionable garden parties, gala naval balls, May Day celebrations, the pomp of legislative openings, and all the trappings of British fashion became the order of the ruling elite in the city, contributing a veneer of transplanted Victorian society over this growing western city. The crowning touch was the opening of the grandiose Parliament Buildings in 1897, the Diamond Jubilee Year of Queen Victoria.

City traditions recall an era of gracious living: afternoon tea in the Empress lobby; old-fashioned Victoria Day celebrations; Chinese New Year; garden receptions at Government House; military tattoos on the lawn before the Parliament Buildings; Tally-Ho horse-drawn tours of the city; the arrival of ships in the Inner Harbour and the ceremonial "Speech from the Throne" by the Queen's representative the Lieutenant-Governor; and countless other political, social and sporting events.

Though long past its heyday, the Port of Victoria still echoes with the whistles of the B.C. Steamship's "Princess Marguerite", the Black Ball ferry "Coho", visiting cruise liners, naval ships, coast guard patrol vessels and the gargantuan tugs of Seaspan's ocean fleet, seiners and trollers of the salmon fleet, cargo freighters from around the world, and the summer crush of yachts from around the Pacific coast. The dramatic Swiftsure Race down the straits to the open Pacific and back to Victoria is an annual racing classic attracting hundreds of the northwest's fastest yachts in May of each year.

Today, the City of Victoria, with a population of 66,000 is part of a large metropolitan area with a total population of slightly less than 260,000 people. The neighbouring municipalities of Esquimalt, Oak Bay, and Saanich blend into Victoria so unobtrusively that visitors, and sometimes residents are not aware of passing from one to another.

INTEREST SPOTS

Victoria's claim to beauty and style are well founded; the city boasts an abundance of attractive and historic features. Some of the most prominent are: the palatial neo-gothic Parliament Buildings overlooking the Inner Harbour; the chateau-styled Empress Hotel; Bastion Square and Centennial Square; the ever-popular import and antique shops; venerable cathedrals; flower-potted street lamps; windy Beacon Hill Park; the enigmatic totems of Thunderbird Park; the new Provincial Museum in Heritage Court; beautifully restored McPherson Playhouse and the City Hall; historic Old Town, Chinatown and the Gorge Waterway; and countless attractive homes, parks, and viewpoints.

THE INNER HARBOUR

This has always been the central focus of Victoria: Here the trading vessels, sealing and fishing fleets, world clippers, and C.P.R. steamships docked at the city's doorstep. On the Causeway at the harbour's edge, bronze plaques commemorate historic vessels that called Victoria their home port.

James Bay, as it is named on the charts, was blocked by the construction of the granite seawall and causeway in 1906. The area behind was filled and now supports the Empress Hotel, Crystal Gardens, and lawn bowling greens.

Leading 3½ miles northwestward, from the harbour into Portage Inlet is the narrow Gorge Waterway, a natural tidal channel that was once the new colony's major transport access to and from the fort. Many of the first homes and farms, such as Point Ellice house and Craigflower Manor, were located near its banks.

Indian canoe races were a popular feature of the harbour regatta in 1904.

56

The helpful staff in the tourist office at the inner harbour, can direct you to anything anywhere. Get a good city and island map. Be sure and check if any special events are taking place during your visit. Here are some features and their stories, briefly, to whet your curiosity. Good touring.

PARLIAMENT BUILDINGS

The massive granite Parliament Buildings are outstanding in architecture and setting. Designed in the neo-gothic style popular for many edifices of Victorian England, these splendid buildings were opened in 1897 and dedicated to Queen Victoria on the occasion of Her Majesty's Diamond Jubilee—Victoria's button-bursting offering to a world-wide celebration.

Costing $923,000 and constructed with B.C. stone and wood over a period of four years, the Parliament Buildings feature sweeping hallways of carved panelling and leaded glass artwork, vaulted chambers where the Legislature sits below public galleries, a muralled rotunda under the central dome, and a stately library with reading rooms. The crowning touch is the copper-coated central dome topped with the golden statue of Captain Vancouver.

Regular weekday tours are conducted from the information office inside the front entrance. A walk around the outside is equally worthwhile; there are statues, cupolas and various embellishments on the building, and quiet formal gardens and lawns gracing its setting.

HERITAGE COURT

Here is the focus for the whole museum/archive complex next to the Parliament Buildings. Bells peal over the Court's entrance from the 90 foot Carillon Tower, a Centennial gift from the Dutch community. The tower's mirror image lies on a broad still pool in a sunken garden, the entrance to the Provincial archives. The garden itself blooms with wildflowers and shrubbery collected painstakingly from all regions of the province.

Victoria's Inner Harbour — the Strait of Juan de Fuca beyond.

The Archives and the Curatorial Tower behind hoard national and cultural treasures, manuscripts, photographs, journals, specimens, samples, bones, and scientific bric a brac; an invaluable research and custodial centre.

Entrance to Heritage Court from Thunderbird Park leads through a covered arcade. Here the ghostly spirits of earlier histories peer out from old, sombre weather-torn totem poles and canoes granted historical respite and shelter from the elements. The opposite end of the Court leads off through "Colombo Place" to the Parliament Buildings, past gaunt abstract sculptures, images of the present and the future.

PROVINCIAL MUSEUM

The Museum is a showplace of natural and human British Columbia history with a collection dating back to the museum's founding in 1887.

Orientation Hall on the main floor features streaming curtains of water, almost unbelievable in construction and acting like a veil between us and the past. Behind, a giant 30 foot carving of a dugout canoe with eight life-size Nootka whalers with harpoons poised in pursuit of a Gray whale.

The "First Peoples" exhibit upstairs, explores the native Indian view of natural and supernatural life. Full scale home models, a cedar Kwakiutl longhouse and an underground pit-house clearly contrast the coastal and interior Indian lifestyles. They are complete with the fascinating artifacts of ceremonial and household activities: storage chests made of bent wood, Chilkat blankets woven with animal fibres, hunting and fishing tools, weapons and "slave killers", and the many distinctive masks used in dancing and storytelling.

"Living Land, Living Sea", the new natural history exhibit uses dramatic techniques that draw visitors deep into a coastal forest where a grizzly bear fishes in a stream bed and elk rest in the forest shade. Then to the seashore, alongside basking sea lions, nesting birds and foraging waterfowl. Very realistic.

The "Contemporary Man" exhibit depicts the settlement of British Columbia and the artifacts of "modernity". Visitors will find themselves back in a pioneer town complete with furnished shops, hotel, theatre and train station. Or they can examine a coal mine shaft, upcoast fish cannery, a Peace River farm, or slip into Captain Vancouver's private cabin on his ship "Discovery." The museum is free and open daily.

Clearly, the range and inventiveness of the museum's exhibits should put it high on a visitor's "must see" list. The museum is open daily, and free.

THUNDERBIRD PARK

Probably the world's finest collection of totem poles, these great sky-reaching poles, heavy in art and symbolism, are a distinctive tribute to the great Indian cultures along the northwest coast. They represent the Nootka, Salish, Kwakiutl, Bella Coola, Haida, and Tsimshian peoples. The park also has a ceremonial longhouse decorated with a traditional Kwakiutl motif, and a busy carving shed where craftsmen make new poles and replicas of old decayed ones. Additional totem poles, canoes, and carvings are housed next door in the Provincial Museum.

For centuries before its discovery by Europeans, the natural richness of the northwest coast supported a large population of native Indian people. Isolated by great mountain ranges and the broad ocean, they independently developed an advanced and complex society, rich in natural and spiritual heritage. Their culture found its most striking expression in the great carved columns of cedar commonly called totem poles.

Totem poles dramatically attest to the vigor and imagination of coastal Indian cultures and give an exciting glimpse into their complex mythology and social organization. Carved for powerful and wealthy men to erect before their homes, or family lodges, the totem affirmed the owner's social rank, family crest, heritage, and perhaps special family traditions or mythology. This was depicted by stylized animal forms such as the bear, beaver, killer whale, eagle, or the raven. Some carvings, such as the Thunderbird, are purely mythical; others are half-man, half-beast. Symbolic "coppers" and little potlach men signified wealth and power. Every figure on the pole has special meaning and value in the totem of the family owning the pole. Upon completion, the totem pole was raised during a prolonged celebration or potlach.

This system of "heraldry" reached its zenith after the arrival of traders who introduced new materials, tools, weapons, and trading markets. The fur trade propelled Indian societies towards new heights of competition, power, and wealth, all

The provincial museum with part of Thunderbird Park in the foreground.

The Nootka whaling scene in the museum's main hall.

reflected vigorously in their art. Most totem poles·in the park are authentic replicas of poles carved between 1850 and 1890, the zenith of coast Indian art, and the apex of power and greatness for the large coast Indian nations. After this period, the Indian cultures went into serious dislocation and decline and Totem carving became a fast-disappearing art.

Today the stylized grotesque poles of the Kwakiutl from around Alert Bay are leading a strong revival of this art. New poles can now be seen throughout the Island—in parks, at viewpoints, and once again on Indian land. But there is no finer standing collection than those at Thunderbird Park.

EMPRESS HOTEL

This is the most stately and charming hotel in the province, and has been the cornerstone of Victoria society and a mecca for world travellers since its opening in 1908. The "chateau"-styled hotel was designed by Francis Rattenbury, architect of the Parliament Buildings and several other prominent buildings. Favorite daughter of the C.P.R. Hotel chain, the Empress was furnished to match any of the best hostelries of Europe and embellished with an elegant ballroom, adjoining conservatory, and rose gardens. Famous for its traditions, the Empress daily features afternoon tea and crumpets in the lobby.

CRYSTAL GARDENS

From baby shows to world swimming records to wartime parachute training — the Garden has seen it all. Here generations of Victorians learned to swim, enjoy flower shows and exhibitions, or gathered regularly for big band dancing.

Designed in the tradition of the great glass halls of Europe and opened in 1925, a conservatory combined with the largest saltwater pool in the British Empire, it was host to a wide range of leisure activities under the soaring glass roof.

Closed in 1971 due to high maintenance costs, it was reopened in 1980 due to an outpouring of protest from heritage-conscious citizens. Once again, residents and visitors enjoy afternoon tea in the Victorian tradition, on the promenade overlooking the lush garden, with its cascading waterfalls, tropical birds and plants.

Government Street in 1906, looking north at the corner of Broughton.

BASTION SQUARE

Here is the reclaimed heart of "Old Town"—a collection of former warehouses, offices, saloons, provincial courthouse, and waterfront hotels of occasionally dubious reputation now dressed up as boutiques, art galleries, offices, restaurants, and the Maritime Museum. The site was originally occupied by one of the military bastions of Fort Victoria, (page 38). Most of the buildings are from the city's boom days of more than a century ago.

MARITIME MUSEUM

This is the final proud home of the brave little "Tillicum", a converted Indian dug-out canoe which sailed in 1901 from Victoria into the vast Pacific, London bound. Her captain Voss attracted world-wide attention for his bravery and his unique sturdy vessel. Years later Tillicum was found still in London, aground and neglected on the Thames bank. She was quickly returned to her home port, to a heroine's welcome, and a place of honour in our maritime history.

The Tillicum, figureheads, scrimshaw, bow badges, uniforms, ship models, and maritime equipment—the Maritime Museum holds a fascinating collection. It roughly covers the coastal shipping and fishing history, the years of the Royal British Navy Fleet in the Pacific, and the development of the Canadian Navy. There is also a fascinating ancient "cage elevator" to the top floor library and workshop.

The Maritime Museum occupies the former Provincial Court House, an imposing turreted building of 1889 vintage, on Bastion Square. Open Daily.

As you tour the city and surrounding municipalities there are other attractions you may find of interest. The renovated MacPherson Playhouse theatre and the re-vitalized Victoria City Hall ring the fountains and courts around Centennial Square. Over several blocks and centred on Fisgard Street are the remnants of Chinatown, once one of the largest on Vancouver Island, and now the last.

You may also want to explore shady Trounce Alley leading to Bastion Square, or Fan Tan Alley leading into Chinatown. Christ Church Cathedral, the city's largest church, is next to

Pioneer Park, the city's oldest gravesite. Government House and its manicured public gardens out on swank Rockland Crescent and Fisherman's Wharf in James Bay may also prove of interest. Many downtown streets have blooming flower-baskets on the old English street lamps.

A short trip by car will also take you to Victoria's centres of "higher learning", Camosun College and the University of Victoria. You may enjoy a visit to the Astrophysical Observatory on Saanich Mountain, or the Gonzales Hill Observatory and nearby Walburn Park with its commanding view of the Strait of Juan de Fuca and the Navigators' Memorial plaque with its lengthy narrative about the Strait's discovery.

Beginning at the Inner Harbour you can take a marine drive around James Bay to Ogden Point past Beacon Hill Park and on through Oak Bay, past Cadboro Bay and finally onto Cordova Bay. There are many viewpoints on this drive where you will have a sweeping view of the ocean and the Olympic Mountains of Washington State.

For a day's outing, the Victoria to Sooke Highway or the Saanich peninsula have many varied attractions. See the Milestone Guide on page 133 or page 151.

Via Rail runs a daily passenger service on the E.&N. Railroad. A 140 mile, scenic run up the east coast of the Island to Courtenay. Leaves Victoria at 8:10 AM, returning at 5:20 PM. This is an easy way to enjoy a day's outing. There is no food on board, so bring a lunch.

While in Victoria, take a walking tour of the waterfront and the streets abounding it. You will find a wealth of shops and eateries, many are housed in old and historic buildings that date back to the 1860's.

The Emily Carr Gallery, with its large collection of her paintings and books, and the Provincial Tourist Bureau, both on Wharf Street, are well worth a visit.

Looking for a park to relax, have a picnic and let the children work off some energy? There are a number to be found, enquire at the Tourist Bureau. Here are a few.

BEACON HILL PARK

The most colourful and beloved park in the Victoria area got its name because of a very dangerous submerged reef lying off-shore. Brotchie Ledge caused several shipwrecks in the early days of Fort Victoria, before its position was indicated to mariners by directional markers and beaconfires on the hill.

When the first white settlers arrived in the 1840s they found the knoll and slopes dotted with pre-historic burial mounds. This area was the first in the entire province to be set aside as a park. It was so designated by the Hudson's Bay Company in the late 1850s but had been used as such for over ten years. Ever since the early settlers gathered to play or celebrate, this convenient and beautiful spot has been a cherished part of community life. The cricket field for example has been in use for over one hundred years. Horse racing was another sport of those distant times.

There is a very happy blending of the picturesque natural scene with artificial ponds, shady green lawns, and bright flower beds. Daffodils in the thousands spring from the verdant grass. This display is followed by the purple sheen of meadows of camas winding through the brilliant gold broom.

Garry oak trees grace many lovely homes in the area.

65

Through spring and summer a succession of flowers and shrubs keep the park gay and attractive. Of particular note are the polyanthus, pansies, and tulips of May, the rhododendrons, and azaleas of late May, and the lively rose gardens during summer months.

Mile 1 of the 4,860 mile Trans Canada Highway starts here at Beacon Hill, by the sweeping cliffs on the Pacific Ocean. It ends at St. John's in Newfoundland, at the edge of the Atlantic Ocean; "ad mari usque ad mare" is our national motto, and this is certainly a spot to ponder over such a vastness.

The park fronts on the ocean and from Beacon Hill or vantage points along Dallas Road, a superb view is possible across the 16-mile Juan de Fuca Strait, to the snow-capped backdrop of the Olympic Mountains in Washington State.

MT. TOLMIE and MT. DOUGLAS PARK

These hills in Saanich offer excellent viewpoints overlooking the city. The former is closer to downtown Victoria and allows a close-up view of the city; the latter is a large, well-forested park. Mt. Douglas, the taller, affords a wide panorama of the whole Saanich peninsula, Haro Strait, and the Gulf Islands, Juan de Fuca Strait, and the Olympic mountains beyond. A viewpoint directory names prominent features on the horizon and a "stop-of-interest" plaque explains the history of Victoria's growth. The park also includes a beach for swimming, or picnicking, and miles of hiking trails through the forest.

The Kinsmen Gorge Park by Tillicum Road is an excellent spot for picnics and walking the waterway's banks.

VICTORIA ART GALLERY

The Art Gallery holds works by prominent Vancouver Island artists such as Herbert Siebner, Maxwell Bates, and Fleming Jorgensen. The nationally eminent Group of Seven, and Victoria's own Emily Carr, all noted for their impressive visions of Canadian backcountry, are also well represented. Miss Carr's austere paintings of early Indian villages and deep wind-swept west coast forests propelled her into world-wide fame.

The Gallery is at 1040 Moss Street in the elegant "Spencer House", just east of downtown, and open daily.

HISTORIC HOMES

From crude colonial manors to lavish "castled" estates, much of Victoria's past is still well preserved and open to public view. A few are the province's oldest standing structures, some were the most sumptuous, and nearly all are enhanced with interesting displays of furniture, handicrafts, tools, and period arts, and set in gracious gardens. A quiet thoughtful tour of these historic homes reaps a wealth of insight about life in early Victoria and the personal stories behind history.

The Provincial Museum is an excellent complement to touring these old homes and makes a good starting point for a fascinating encounter with local history.

HELMCKEN HOUSE next to the Provincial Museum, is the province's oldest standing residence. It was built in 1852, nine years after the founding of Fort Victoria, by Dr. Helmcken, a German physician and advisor with the Hudson's Bay Company. He later became a prominent political leader in the growing colony.

The house was built with timbers hand-hewn from logs hauled by oxen up from the beach at James Bay. The house grew section by section apace with the doctor's growing family. Many of the original family furnishings and a large display of early medical instruments and medicines complement this rustic old home.

EMILY CARR HOUSE is the 1871 birthplace of British Columbia's most outstanding painter and authoress. Miss Carr's father had the home built in 1863 on a ten-acre plot using stout California redwood timbers. The recently renovated house remains a sturdy example of mid-Victorian family design. It is located at 207 Government Street, only a few blocks past the Parliament Buildings.

Emily Carr's last years as an artist were spent at her sister's home only a block away, where she culminated a lifetime of study in art and writing. She created a compassionate and bold new image of the west coast forests and Indian villages, and her paintings are now national treasures, found in collections throughout Canada and Europe.

CRAIGFLOWER MANOR AND SCHOOLHOUSE were part of Craigflower Farm, one of the earliest agricultural settlements on Vancouver Island and one of four operated by the Puget Sound Agricultural Company, a subsidiary of the Hudson's Bay Company. The farm supplied dairy and farm produce to the young colony and maintained a sawmill, flour mill, bakery, kilns, smithy, and general store. The farm was begun in 1853 by Ken McKenzie, a company bailiff brought from England with twenty-four other families. The site they chose had open glades for grazing cattle and convenient access via the Gorge waterway to the fort at the harbour.

The Emily Carr home has been preserved as a National Historic site.

Craigflower Manor itself is a solid monument to the skills and workmanship of the early settlers in the new colony. It was built in 1856 almost entirely of locally produced timber, clay brick, and ironwork. The massive iron-studded oak doors and strong window shutters made the house defensible if attacked.

But fortunately one never came. McKenzie made the manor a popular social centre and a favourite call of British naval officers ashore from their ships at anchor in nearby Esquimalt Harbour.

Today only the manor and schoolhouse remain as reminders of the early company farm; both are designated as national historic sites. Craigflower Manor is fully furnished and colourfully decorated in the style of early colonial life. The schoolhouse, too, is a museum. Scarred old desks and solemn class portraits fill the room of the oldest schoolhouse west of the Great Lakes. Craigflower is on Highway 1A by its junction with Admiral's Road, and can be found by using the Milestone Guide on page 152.

POINT ELLICE HOUSE built in 1861 on the banks of the Gorge, was home of the colonial Gold Commissioner and Judge, Peter O'Reilly, who presided over the Kootenay goldfields and later rose to political prominence at the capital. Point Ellice House three generations later still in family hands, contains his original rich furnishings and household effects. This gracious home is an "oasis of mid-Victorian charm" on a quiet gardened estate at 2616 Pleasant Street. Turn off Bay Street at the eastern end of Point Ellice Bridge.

CRAIGDARROCH CASTLE is an impressive testimony to the wealthy Vancouver Island coal baron, Robert Dunsmuir. Originally one of the founding coal miners employed at Fort Rupert and Nanaimo by the Hudson's Bay Company, Dunsmuir later developed his own coal strikes which became the foundation of his massive fortune. In the process he became the industrial captain of the Island's development and builder of the first railroad, the Esquimalt and Nanaimo R.R.

When he finally moved to Victoria, Dunsmuir directed his architect to recreate a Scottish castle for his family home—cost was no consideration. It was to be a majestic showpiece for a very wealthy family: the social lions of Victoria.

Austere and turreted, the massive four-story castle features huge stone hearths, curved stained-glass windows, and grand rooms that once hosted the elite of Victoria society.

Robert Dunsmuir unfortunately died just as his great home was completed in 1889. He never saw the great balls and receptions his large, proud family held at the estate. James Douglas, his scion and heir to the industrial and family throne,

Robert Dunsmuir's Craigdarroch Castle.

eventually became Premier, and later Lieutenant Governor of British Columbia and built the Hatley Park estate. See page 154.

Today the imposing castle is home to the Victoria Conservatory of Music. Its location, at 1050 Joan Crescent, is just off

Fort Street to the east of downtown Victoria, and is open daily for viewing.

Many of greater Victoria's byways and sidestreets are also adorned by older gracious homes; many are equally as famous locally as the aforementioned. Government House, Spencer House, and certainly Hatley Park are also of superb distinction.

Victoria and its surrounding municipalities offer many more sights and interest spots than can be squeezed into this book. There are besides many sporting, cultural, military, and political activities that further illustrate the fabric of the city. If you have

A great way to explore Victoria, the Saanich Peninsula and many other areas of the Island.

time you may want to explore the markets, nightspots, industries, churches, parks, and academies that make up the community.

The attractions outlined have been only the more distinguished and popular features of a colourful and historic capital city; hopefully your curiosity has been aroused to explore further.

The modern highway over the Malahat Ridge.

Beginning of the Trans-Canada Highway at the south end of Victoria's Douglas Street.

Victoria to Duncan

THE western terminus of the Trans-Canada Highway is located at the southwest corner of Victoria's Beacon Hill Park. This 4,860 mile highway stretches across Canada's 10 provinces, linking Victoria with St. John's, Newfoundland. The highway was begun in 1950, cost $1 billion and was officially opened in 1962. Designated #1, it proceeds (via Douglas Street) north to Nanaimo and then (by ferry) to Horseshoe Bay on the mainland.

Mileage figures in brackets are for the convenience of those travelling south from Duncan to Victoria.

0.0 (35.2) JUNCTION: Our Milestone Guide commences three miles north where a directional sign indicates "turn right" for Highway 17 and Swartz Bay and straight ahead for No. 1 and up-island. It is interesting to note, that in the 1920s, it took about five hours to drive from Victoria to Nanaimo, an easy one and a half to two hours today. Highway 17 serves the Saanich Peninsula and the B.C. Ferry Terminal at Swartz Bay. This 17-mile route is detailed in the Milestone Guide on page 133.

3.5 (31.7) JUNCTION: This is an access to Highways 1A and 14, The Victoria/Sooke/Port Renfrew route that is detailed in the Milestone Guide on page 151. A number of interesting features: Fort Rodd Hill, which is a National Historic Site; Royal Roads Botanical Gardens (Hatley Park); the Esquimalt Lagoon and Royal Colwood Golf Course are all located within two miles by turning off here. The nearby Colwood shopping centre has a variety of services to offer. You can then rejoin Highway No. 1 about four miles north of Colwood.

4.2 (31.0) THETIS LAKE PARK is a very popular recreation area comprising 1630 acres of woodland with numerous hiking trails. In season, there are change rooms, toilets, a food concession and picnic tables. The swimming facilities are not too good for small children, so care should be exercised, for there are no lifeguards.

7.9 (27.3) HIGHWAY 1A is the alternative older route to and from downtown Victoria through Colwood. Many excellent motels are concentrated along this road.

8.8 (26.4) GOLDSTREAM PROVINCIAL PARK is crossed by the Island highway, giving easy access to Victoria as well as up-island points for those using this camping area. The entrance to the campground is down the side road at this junction. The picnic site and area to park while exploring, is one mile north. 173 campsites and 43 picnic sites together with a "sani-station" for trailers are provided. In the summer a park naturalist is in attendance to conduct nature walks and talks. A number of trails take you through a wealth of flora typical of southern British Columbia.

November is the time of one of nature's most important events in the Goldstream River—the return of the coho salmon from the ocean to spawn and die. This completes a cycle that began three years previously when the young fry, after a short time in the river, took to the ocean to mature and grow.

The river was first called Gold Creek by Peter Leech, a prospector who discovered gold here in 1885. Old shafts and tunnels can still be found along the Ridge Trail.

The Ridge Trail takes you to Niagara Creek and the top of Niagara Falls, a spectacular 100-foot cascade. For safety sake, great care should be taken while viewing the falls. You can then proceed down the trail to the highway, a short distance north of the parking area.

10.9 (24.3) BOAT LAUNCHING facilities are available at this private marina, or you can rent a boat and tackle to try your luck at fishing for salmon in the Finlayson Arm of the Saanich Inlet.

THE MALAHAT: As we use this 10 mile section of modern highway it is interesting to consider the travelling conditions of earlier days. Until the 1860s movement to up-island points from Victoria was by water, with some primitive wagon trails from landing points to nearby farms and small settlements. The pressing need for a means of overland movement, especially for farm stock, was recognized by the colonial officials at Victoria and in 1861 a trail five feet wide was constructed from Victoria to Cowichan Bay. Called the Goldstream Trail, it was, to quote the Colonist paper of October 24, 1861, "To be used for stock first, then it is to be made into a wagon road next year." However, the record shows that it remained a trail suitable only for stock and those afoot or on horseback until 1884, when it finally became a rough wagon road—twenty-three years later.

Located west of the present road, it suffered from neglect and travellers complained about fallen trees and flooded areas. It was not until the early 1900s that construction of a road over the Malahat Ridge commenced. It opened for traffic in June of 1911 at a completion cost of $297,249.99. The nature of the job can best be appreciated by the fact that eighteen bridges and one hundred and twenty-three culverts had to be constructed in the ten miles.

Reconstructed in 1925, the traffic increase through the years had made continual improvement necessary and you can now travel from Victoria to Cowichan Bay in an easy half hour or so. In the days of the trail it was a two- and sometimes three-day trip.

15.9 (19.3) SOUTH JUNCTION TO SHAWNIGAN LAKE: While this is a pleasant drive, a more direct route to the lake is about eight miles farther north.

16.5 (18.7) SPECTACLE LAKE is a short distance west of the highway. A delightful area with a good walking trail around the lake for a ramble, or to try your luck at casting for trout. There are picnic tables and toilets and you can have a refreshing swim before continuing your journey. Observe the shape of the lake to see how it got its name.

Pioneer autoist tackling the Malahat summit about 1912.

17.1 (18.1) MALAHAT SUMMIT: An elevation of 1,156 feet gives you an outstanding view to the south of the Saanich Inlet's Finlayson Arm and the mountains of the Olympic Peninsula in Washington State.

18.5 (16.7) ARBUTUS REST AREA with picnic tables and toilets.

19.0 (16.2) HISTORICAL STOP OF INTEREST: From 1,000 feet above the Saanich Inlet you look directly at Haro Strait and the southern end of the Strait of Georgia, virtually a "sea of Islands" with the International Boundary running down Haro Strait, separating the Gulf Islands from the San Juan Islands in the United States.

Mt. Baker, 75 miles away "as the crow flies" can be seen rising east of Bellingham, Washington, to 10,778 feet. A favourite skiing area of the northwest, Mt. Baker is a dormant volcano snow-capped the year round.

BAMBERTON CEMENT WORKS: Built in 1912 and now closed, this plant in the 60 years it operated, produced over ten million tons of cement. Previous to 1912 the plant was on the site of what is now Butchart Gardens across the Saanich Inlet.

20.8 (14.4) BAMBERTON BEACH PARK is another of the excellent Provincial Parks providing salt-water swimming, 50 campsites, 39 picnic sites and a Sani-station.

THE MILL BAY FERRY is one mile east of the main highway. This twenty-minute ferry trip to Brentwood Bay on the Saanich Peninsula is an alternate route to and from Greater Victoria.

MILL BAY ROAD skirts the shore and then rejoins the main highway three miles north. This is part of the original Island Highway, and less than half a mile beyond the ferry landing will be found a roadside spring producing a steady stream of cold water. The catch basin carries the words, "Victoria Rotary Club 1924". This relic of the past gives mute evidence of a service rendered in the days when the radiator had to be filled to the brim before the car could tackle the climb up the Malahat.

23.9 (11.3) MILL BAY: One of the earliest sawmills on the Island was built here in 1861 by a Mr. Shepard. He sold out later that year to William Sayward, who became quite a lumbering magnate on the Island. Sayward forest and the village of Sayward north of Campbell River still perpetuate his name. His unskilled millworkers were paid $1.00 for a twelve-hour day, plus room and board.

There is an interesting sidelight on the area. The nearby Shawnigan Lake Lumber Company's opening entries in their journal, dated February 1894, read: "7½ yoke of oxen (15 animals) and logging outfit $3,000.00." "Wages for swampers, skidroad men, drivers and riggers $35.00 per month and board, fallers and buckers $40.00 and board". Today's fallers will earn yearly approximately $54,000 and riggers $35,000.

24.1 (11.1) SHAWNIGAN CREEK served the mill down on the bay. Along its bank a "skid road" was used for hauling logs by oxen and a 1,500-foot flume carried water from up-stream to the millwheel, providing power to drive the saws.

Eight yoke of oxen hauling logs out of the bush in the 1890s.

24.2 (11.0) SHAWNIGAN LAKE is four miles west of the highway and is a popular summer cottage area for many Victorians. It has little public access except for boat launching, plus a 53 unit picnic park.

24.8 (10.4) ST. FRANCIS XAVIER CHURCH: A short distance east on Kilmalu Road, is a good example of the early pioneer churches that served the first settlers. St. Francis was built in 1887 by volunteer labour under the direction of Father Donckele.

28.5 (6.7) JUNCTION: The community of Cobble Hill is one and a half miles southwest of here. The road then continues to Shawnigan Lake and returns to the main highway five miles south of this junction. This is part of the original meandering Island Highway, which you can follow east from this junction to Cowichan Bay, thence north to Maple Bay, Crofton, and Chemainus. Designated 1A, it rejoins the main highway at Ladysmith 23 miles north of this junction. A very pleasant side trip via this route is outlined in the Milestone Guide on page 167.

29.2 (6.0) DOUGAN'S LAKE: A small circular lake that offers fair fishing during spring and fall, but which has limited access for parking and boat launching.

32.0 (3.0) WHIPPLETREE JUNCTION: A recreated turn-of-the-century village with restored buildings, some from Duncan's old Chinatown. In addition to the craft shops, there are incredible collections of artifacts and antiques. Across the highway is the Glass Castle, built in 1962 with a collection of over 180,000 bottles.

32.7 (2.5) COWICHAN GOLF & COUNTRY CLUB: An 18-hole course with an impressive backdrop provided by Mt. Tzouhalem to the east. Read the fascinating story about this mountain on page 171.

33.2 (2.0) JUNCTION: Four miles east to Cowichan Bay.

33.8 (1.4) PICNIC SITE.

33.9 (1.3) COWICHAN INDIAN SWEATERS: When early explorers reached the shores of the Pacific Northwest they found artistic natives very proficient in carving and weaving. Shawls, robes and blankets were skillfully woven using cedar bark, reeds, dog hair and the wool of mountain goats mixed with duck down and cotton from fireweed and other plants to give a finer quality to the garment. The fine "Chilkat" blankets worn by Indian leaders became popular in Europe.

These inherited skills of the Cowichan Indian women have been adapted to the knitting methods of today in creating the unique "Cowichan" sweater. Made from naturally coloured raw wool and containing the original lanolin oil, they are attractive, rain-resistant, warm and long wearing. Like the first Indian-crafted blankets given in trade these Cowichan sweaters have found world-wide popularity.

34.5 (0.7) KOKSILAH FOREST NURSERY is a provincial forestry project where seeds extracted from cones of select healthy trees are "set-out" to germinate in the nursery. After two years these seedlings are planted in logged-off areas, and are ready for harvest in approximately 80 to 100 years. Roughly eight million seedlings a year are produced at Koksilah under close genetic quality control. The public is welcome to make enquiries.

34.9 (0.3) THE COWICHAN RIVER flows east from Cowichan Lake. About 28 miles long, it is one of the best and most consistent fish producing rivers on Vancouver Island. Brown, cutthroat, rainbow, and steelhead trout are available all year round but mid-summer activity is slow.

Sport shops in Duncan can provide suitable tackle and access information for fishing the River and other nearby lakes and rivers.

35.2 (0.0) JUNCTION: Duncan city centre is one half mile to the west on Trunk Road. The road east takes you to Maple Bay, Crofton, and Chemainus. See the Milestone Guide on page 172.

The Duncan Tourist Information Bureau is located one-half block north of this junction.

Highway 18 to Cowichan Lake can be taken through Duncan City centre, or by way of a junction three miles north on the main highway. This route is detailed in the Milestone Guide on page 177.

DUNCAN: Population 4,391. This pleasant little city serves the large farming and forestry community of the Cowichan Valley. It is believed that the word Cowichan means "warmed by the sun" and certainly the valley gets a full share of sunshine. Duncan has a dual personality: in one aspect it is the heart of a major lumbering and logging area; in another it is a paradise for gardeners, farmers and sports fishermen.

In 1886, a group of the area's settlers met and petitioned the E & N Railway to establish a station at the point where the railway ran through a farm owned by William C. Duncan. That same year a townsite was laid out on Mr. Duncan's land

and the first home was built where the Tzouhalem Hotel now stands. The new community was first called Duncan's Farm then changed to Alderley, the name of the farm. Subsequently it became Duncan's Crossing, Duncan's Station, Duncan's and finally it was incorporated as Duncan in 1912.

Mileage figures in brackets are for the convenience of those travelling south from Duncan to Victoria.

High-lead logging in earlier days. The tree left standing and rigged for this operation is about 150 feet high, judging by the size of the man on the rail car.

Retired from service in the logging industry, this steam locomotive intrigues visitors to the Forest Museum near Duncan.

Duncan to Nanaimo

THIS direct route to Nanaimo is through areas of small farms and rural residential settlements but by-passes some small villages, that are still served by the old island highway. See map 4.

Mileage figures in brackets are for the convenience of those travelling south from Nanaimo to Duncan.
To convert to Kilometers, multiply by 1.6.

0.0 (31.5) JUNCTION of Highway 1 and Trunk Road.
MT. PREVOST can be seen west of the highway. It rises 2,600 feet above sea level, and is named after Capt. James Charles Prevost, R.N., one of the many British Navy officers on this coast in the 1860s. On the mountain top is a 36-foot column of granite, a memorial to the 1914-18 war dead of the Cowichan Valley. A plaque with the names of the fallen during the second World War was added.

1.5 (30.0) SOMENOS LAKE: This small lake set in rich farm-lands was mentioned in the British Colonist newspaper of Victoria under the date of November 26, 1862: "The sloop "Louisa" sailed for Cowichan last night with six passengers, a quantity of provisions, etc., for the settlers. One of the settlers, who has a fine location on Somenos Lake, a short distance above the Cowichan River, is taking up nine or ten head of cattle, and intends establishing a dairy farm, for which the settlement is particularly adapted."

2.0 (29.5) FOREST MUSEUM: Originally started as a private venture by a Gerry Wellburn, and now operated by the Provincial Government, "Man In The Forest" is the theme of this excellent attraction. Over 100 acres of indoor and outdoor exhibits, showing how the logging and lumbering industry has evolved from the early days of water-wheel powered sawmills and primitive logging methods to today's modern systems. The crowning touch is an exciting train ride behind a steam locomotive on the narrow guage railway that circles the park. This is one of the most popular attractions on the Island with lots of exhibits to interest young and old. Visitors leave with a better understanding of our forest heritage and the importance of our proper use and protection of it.

3.0 (23.5) JUNCTION: West to Lake Cowichan. See the Milestone Guide beginning on page 177.

7.2 (24.3) JUNCTION: East to Crofton and the Saltspring Island ferry. See page 173.

7.6 (23.9) THE CHEMAINUS RIVER is not too productive for sport fishing. Late spring is best for trout and some steelhead are taken during mid-winter.

9.5 (22.0) FULLER LAKE is a short distance east of the highway and provides an excellent place for a picnic and swim. The lake has been stocked with rainbow trout and there are boat launching facilities. Tennis courts are available.

9.9 (21.6) HENRY ROAD: Two miles into Chemainus. A "must" trip. See the details on page 174.

16.1 (15.4) JUNCTION: Highway 1A which left the main highway south of Duncan at mile 28.5 rejoins here. The Milestone Guide on page 175 details this route through Chemainus, Maple Bay and Cowichan Bay.

17.3 (14.2) LADYSMITH: Population 4558, was an "instant" town" needed by James Dunsmuir as a site for deep water

First steam donkey in B.C. logging on display at the Forest Museum.

loading of coal from his new coal fields at Extension, 11 miles away by rail. He also needed a community for the miners away from the dust and grime of the mines. Building was undertaken on the heavily timbered slopes in 1898. The big trees were felled and hauled to the waters edge where a wharf and loading facilities were constructed. Less than a year later the first coal was dumped into a waiting ship. The first buildings for the new town were "hand-me-downs". Vacant houses at Wellington, 20 miles north, were sawn into sections, loaded onto rail cars and re-assembled at Ladysmith. Some are still in use to this day. As the demand for coal fell off, the value of the surrounding forests became apparent and logging and lumbering eventually became the main activity. Ladysmith's harbour today is still the scene of cargo ships loading logs for transport to various world markets.

As you enter town, you will find on display an example of the kind of locomotive used at one time to haul logs from the woods to tidewater. It is on the grounds of an arboretum and logging museum that is well worth a visit. Many native and foreign trees are planted throughout the gardens. Nearby is the tourist information centre where you can acquire information on the camping, hiking and fishing in the area. It is interesting to drive around the town to see some of the old buildings that are still in use. Transfer Beach Park down on the shore, offers swimming and picnic facilities. An excellent place to relax.

THE 49th PARALLEL runs through Ladysmith. This is the famous invisible boundary line between Canada and the United States. Running West into the Strait of Georgia, however, it swings southward to encompass the complete mass of Vancouver Island within Canada. It took some hard-nosed bargaining to agree to this. Otherwise much of Vancouver Island would be in the United States for Ladysmith is 54 miles north of Victoria and the Island's southern shore.

19.6 (11.9) STZUMINUS PARK: 51 campsites, 31 picnic sites and swimming are features of this excellent park operated by the Chemainus Indian Tribe.

20.0 (11.5) PICNIC SITE.

23.2 (8.3) GRANBY: "A vanished community"
Turn west onto Spruston Road, through the railroad underpass and almost immediately you will be on the site of Granby, a coal mining town built in 1917 and deserted in 1936.

Mine buildings and town were built at a cost of one and a half million dollars by the Granby Consolidated Mining and Smelting Company to provide coal for their up-coast copper smelter.

For a population of 700 people, Granby had all the amenities of a modern town: a water and sewerage system, street lighting, school, church, department store, movie theatre, and a 72-room hotel.

Two hundred men working underground produced 1,000 tons of coal in an eight hour shift. The price of copper fell drastically in the 30s, and when the smelter at Anyox was closed in 1935, attempts were made to find other markets for coal, but the shift to oil was reducing the market, and by 1936 Granby was a deserted town.

Many of the finer homes were sold and moved to new sites, but much of the town was left for time and nature to take over. Today you can still see the remains of some wooden structures and the concrete foundations and walls of the mine buildings. Here and there a few fruit trees and shrubs continue to struggle unattended. Much of the town site has now become a gravel pit, and little remains of this once thriving community.

23.7 (7.8) CASSIDY: Long before the advent of Granby, Cassidy's Station on the E & N Railway was the centre of a small settlement at the Nanaimo River crossing. It was named àfter Tom Cassidy who came from Iowa in 1878 and farmed in the area. For many years the Cassidy hotel, built in 1918, was the scene of numerous community activities, and though most of the early community has disappeared, the hotel continues to be a favourite gathering place.

23.9 (7.6) NANAIMO RIVER: This 36 mile river and lake system is one of the prime fishing areas on the Island. The 13 mile paved road brings you to Crown Forest Industries property. The Company office there will provide you with a map of the area, showing the three campsites they have created for public use. Best fishing is April to October for Dolly Varden, cutthroat and Rainbow trout. Do respect the Company's property.

TOURIST INFORMATION CENTRE: Operated in season by the City of Nanaimo. Enquiries here will provide you with information on the many interesting things to do and see in Nanaimo and the surrounding countryside.

25.5 (5.3) MORDEN MINE: Turn east on Morden road, continue to the end of the pavement, about a mile, then a short distance on a dirt road will reveal the last remaining coal mine "tipple" on the Island. Being concrete, it has defied the ravages of time. There is talk of the area being designated as a Provincial Commemorative Park. Tipples were constructed over mine shafts to contain the machinery to raise men and coal to the surface.

26.0 (5.5) JUNCTION TO SOUTH WELLINGTON: At one time the area of this coal mining town was almost entirely owned by pioneering settlers, Mr. & Mrs. James Beck. They sold their 640 acres to unsuccessful mining interests in 1879, who in turn sold to Robert Dunsmuir, who took out a fortune in coal.

South Wellington had more than its share of troubles. In 1884 a bad underground explosion took the lives of 23 miners; in 1914 a forest fire levelled the town; and, in 1915 a section of one of the workings was flooded with a loss of 21 lives. In its busier days South Wellington had a population of 600 or more; but by 1929 it had dwindled to 200. The mines are closed now and the name South Wellington now refers only to the surrounding farming and residential community.

28.4 (3.1) JUNCTION TO EXTENSION: Westward three and one half miles and situated in a shallow basin ringed by timbered hills, was one of the great coal mining centres of over half a century ago. Slag heaps and old buildings are visible reminders of the area's former black wealth.

Petroglyphs.

Several settlers were farming here when coal was discovered in 1896. The coal field was about three miles long and one mile wide, with an average thickness of eight feet.

Dunsmuir sold the mine in 1910 after "skimming the cream" but work continued until the 1930s. Some of the miners stayed on and today the valley is dotted with small homes and farms between the mountains of waste.

29.4 (2.1) PETROGLYPH PARK: Ancient petroglyphs or rock carvings were first found here by white man over one hundred years ago. These rough carvings were done by earlier men with simple tools perhaps thousands of years ago. Assumed by some to be the work of shamans, the medicine men of the tribes, their locations were likely of special spiritual significance, but their full meaning is not understood.

Petroglyphs can be found from Alaska to the Columbia River area of Oregon. Observe them as a unique expression of the past—and encourage others to respect and protect them.

Further examples of petroglyphs can be seen at the Museum in Nanaimo.

Mileage figures in brackets are for the convenience of those travelling south from Nanaimo to Duncan and Victoria

32.0 (0.0) NANAIMO: The "Hub City". With a metropolitan population of over 47,000, Nanaimo is a distribution centre for a large part of the Island. Modern in appearance and still growing, Nanaimo is nevertheless steeped in history. Incorporation as a city in 1874 makes it the third oldest in British Columbia.

Five separate Indian villages were clustered around the area they called "Snenymo" meaning "where the big tribe dwells" or "a big strong tribe".

They were first visited by Europeans in 1791, when the Spanish Captain Jose Narvaez explored these waterways in the schooner "Saturnina", then came Captain George Vancouver on board the "Discovery" in 1792. Settlement by Europeans did not start until 1851 when Governor Douglas at Victoria sent J.W. McKay on behalf of the Hudson's Bay Company, to investigate coal deposits there which had been brought to their attention by a visiting Indian.

The old Bastion in Nanaimo is now a museum at the junction of Bastion and Front Streets. It can be seen overlooking the harbour at centre right, in the 1875 view below, from what is now Piper Park.

Nanaimo and coal is a great chapter itself in the history of Vancouver Island. September 1852 saw the first shipment of coal, 480 barrels, by the schooner "Cadboro" to Victoria. By 1892 there were ten mines operating in or around Nanaimo, plus the mines farther north at Cumberland. Coal was king for over 75 years and a major factor in the economy and settlement of Nanaimo and other Island communities.

The waning of the coal mines in the late 30s and early 40s however has been balanced by a steady increase in forestry, agriculture, fishing, and tourism. Nanaimo has come a long way since the Bastion was built in 1853. Today it is famous for its annual "bath-tub" race from Nanaimo to Vancouver.

Our mile 32.0 is at the Bastion located on the waterfront in downtown Nanaimo. The nearby small hill is Piper Park, location of the city museum which is worth a visit to learn about the fascinating past of the city. Enquire here or at the Bastion for directions to the tourist bureau where you can learn about the many interesting things to do and see in the area.

The court house in Nanaimo, built in 1895, was designed by Francis Rattenbury, architect for the Empress Hotel and the Parliament Buildings in Victoria.

Certainly the trip to the lookout on 3,366 foot Mt. Benson behind Nanaimo is a rewarding drive; for here is a majestic panoramic view of the Strait of Georgia and the mainland beyond. Inquire at the tourist office for directions.

GABRIOLA ISLAND: A highly recommended side trip to do some beachcombing, gather oysters and visit the unique Malaspina Galleries, a sandstone formation created by wind and wave.

NEWCASTLE ISLAND, just offshore from Nanaimo, and Bowen Park in the city are both ideal for a day of swimming, hiking, or just relaxing.

STRAIT OF GEORGIA is an attractive and broad "inland sea" separating Vancouver Island from the mainland. Varying from 18 to 30 miles in width, and about 125 miles long, it contains some of the most picturesque coastline to be found anywhere. Sheltered from the open Pacific, ringed with vigorous forests, blessed by a mild climate and offering rich lowlands in the river valleys and estuaries, the Strait of Georgia became the centre of British Columbia's burgeoning forestry, farming and fishing industries before the turn of the century.

The Strait is also a sea of islands. To the south it is closed off by the Gulf Islands and the San Juan Islands of the United States. To the north, the "Discovery Group" near Campbell River, form the northern boundary. Along its great length are scattered a variety of islands; low, fertile Hornby, Denman and Lasqueti; massive mountainous Texada, and the Gulf Island group. Many of the islands ring with names given by Spanish explorers: Valdes, Galiano, Gabriola, Saturna, Texada, Quadra, Redonda, Cortes and Hernando.

A Spanish Lieutenant, Eliza, was so impressed with the Strait that he gave it the honourific title, "Gran Canal de Nuestra Senora del Rosario del Marinera", the Great Channel of Our Lady of the Rosary of the Seafarers. The following year Captain Vancouver visited the area, changed its name in honour of his patron, King George III, and added British designations to other islands: Mayne, Pender, Denman, Savary, and Hornby. The largest in the Gulf Island group and certainly the most populated was named "Saltspring", by the Hudson's Bay Company because of the number of salty springs to be found. Originally called

Admiral Island, the name Saltspring received such common usage that it became official.

The climate of this area is one of the most attractive in Canada. Temperature and precipitation levels are often similar to the Mediterranean climate. This is the result of the "rain shadow" created by the high mountains of Vancouver Island, which bear the first onslaught of rain from the wet weather systems brought in from the Pacific with the prevailing westerly winds. The result is milder temperatures, more sunshine, and less rain and snow.

A paradise for sports fishermen and boaters, the Strait offers a marine playground that is unique in North America. Many public and private marine parks and boating and fishing facilities exist around the Strait and its islands. They offer safe moorage, camping, water, sanitation facilities and recreation for the boating and fishing tourist; many are only accessible by sea.

Some day a unique Marine Park may be created of the entire basin. The world famous marine scientist Jacques Ives Cousteau, toured the Georgia basin, and declared the marine park concept imminently desirable, imaginative and entirely feasible.

Nanaimo to Parksville

IN 1886 the road between Nanaimo and Parksville was completed—a twisting, winding, forty mile wagon route that forded the innumerable streams without the convenience of bridges. The trip required six to seven hours with a smart team and democrat.

0.0 NANAIMO: Mileages north to Parksville are clocked from the Bastion on Front Street. Proceed north on Front, left on Comox Road then just two short blocks brings you to Terminal Avenue, (Highway 19). Turn right to go north and up-island.

2.3 DEPARTURE BAY JUNCTION to B.C. Ferry terminal for Horseshoe Bay on the mainland.

5.0 JINGLE POT ROAD: An intriguing name. It is said that it came from the method of signalling in the mines. When the cars of coal were brought to the bottom of the shaft the man in charge pulled on a long rope which "jingled" a pot with a few stones in it at the top of the shaft. This was a signal for the winch operator to start hoisting.

LONG LAKE: Turn east at this junction to enter an excellent swimming and picnic area.

5.4 HISTORICAL STOP OF INTEREST: The story of the discovery of coal in the area in 1869.

WELLINGTON: The Dunsmuir coal empire was firmly established by the large amount of fine grade coal mined in this vicinity from around 1870 to 1900. Wellington was once a large "well-heeled" community boasting a large theatre where many of the great names of vaudeville and stage entertained. Another popular diversion was bicycle racing on one of the finest tracks in the Pacific Northwest. When the mines petered out many of the buildings were moved south to Ladysmith.

5.9 BRANNAN LAKE JUNCTION: One of the finest fishing areas of the Island is reached by this road. There are numerous lakes but access to many of them is by private logging roads. Certainly the ardent fisherman should not pass up this area, but get information from the sport shops in Nanaimo before proceeding into this back country.

8.4 LANTZVILLE JUNCTION: Highway 19A. Take this side road for four miles then rejoin the highway. There are some fine sea views framed by twisting arbutus trees. Lantzville is a small community of homes and motels located on a bench overlooking the entrance to Nanoose Bay. A pleasant drive— watch for a holly farm on your right.

12.0 ARBUTUS GROVE: Some of the finest arbutus (or madrona) to be seen on the Island grow in this area. It is the only broad-leafed evergreen in Canada and is exclusive to the Pacific coast. Found mostly below 1,000 feet altitude, it grows on a variety of sites, from rich bottom lands to almost bare rocky slopes, but is usually found on a dry soil in exposed situations.

13.4 NANOOSE BAY PICNIC SITE.

15.0 NANOOSE: After the original road was built to Parksville in 1886, traffic slowly increased and in 1894 the hotel (still standing) was erected. Just prior to World War I a large sawmill and a blasting powder works were in operation in the area.

HAZARDS OF TRAVEL: An official government report of 1864 discusses the state of the trail from Victoria to Comox and takes a mighty dim view of the area north of Nanaimo: "There would, beyond Nanaimo be very little grazing land, and great risk to cattle from wild beasts. With the exception of a little grazing at Qualicum River I believe there is scarcely a blade of grass from Nanaimo to Comox, and no one would attempt to drive stock through a wild country like this without having some pen or enclosure to protect them at night."

17.0 BEAVER CREEK ROAD: In the 1880s, mail and supplies came to the areas north of Nanaimo by boat from Victoria once every two weeks, and were rowed to farms along the shore. A marked improvement came when a wharf was built at Beaver Creek. From there, the freight was distributed to settlers over the few wagon roads then in existence.

17.6 JUNCTION TO PORT ALBERNI: This bypass of Parksville is only for travellers in a hurry.

18.0 The E.&N. RAILWAY: From time to time you will see the tracks of the Esquimalt & Nanaimo railway. The final link between Victoria and Courtenay was built in 1914. See page 64.

18.6 CRAIG HERITAGE PARK: A collection of fine old buildings, including a small log building built in 1888 and used as a post office until 1912. A good example of log construction.

20.2 RATHTREVOR BEACH PARK: This provincial campground has one of the finest sandy beaches on Vancouver Island. It provides 174 campsites and 80 picnic sites. Sani-stations for trailers are available.

20.5 ENGLISHMAN'S RIVER is nineteen miles long, descending from snowfields high on the Beaufort Range. During the spring and fall months and from mid-January to March fishing is good for Kamloops, steelhead, cutthroat, and rainbow trout averaging one to nine pounds.

22.0 PARKSVILLE: Population 5216. Soon after the road from Nanaimo reached "The River" as the small community was known in 1886, a post office was established under the care of Mr. Nelson Parks, who occupied a small cabin where the community park is now located. Hence the name Parksville came into use.

A tourist information centre is located on the main road near the park entrance. Parksville is a very popular place for summer vacationers and fortunately the community had more than average foresight in setting aside this large park combining a picnic area, playgrounds and access to a marvelous beach. Supplementing the numerous attractions of the district is the annual salmon derby and barbeque in mid-August, which attracts hundreds of visitors.

Many fine commercial facilities are in the area to enhance your stay in Parksville: hotels, motels, and resorts with camping facilities. In addition there are three large provincial campgrounds within a short distance of town.

PORT ALBERNI JUNCTION: Turn west on Highway 4 for Ucluelet, Tofino, Pacific Rim National Park, and Long Beach via the city of Port Alberni. This route is detailed in the Milestone Guide on page 185.

Parksville to Courtenay

IN the early years of settlement the big chunk of wilderness between Nanaimo and Courtenay was simply referred to as "North Nanaimo", for although Parksville had a road connection from the south in 1886 it wasn't extended farther north for ten years.

0.0 PARKSVILLE: Junction of Highway 19 and 4. See map 6.

3.8 HISTORIC CHURCH OF ST. ANNE'S is a pioneer landmark beautifully preserved over the years that was built in 1894 when the Reverend C.E. Cooper came to the district and expressed a wish to erect a church in honour of his mother.

Work "bees" were held and everyone helped. Carefully selected cedar logs were dragged out of the forest by oxen, and raised and fitted by expert axemen. The front gable-end is more than thirty logs high so the framing was no easy task. The church and cemetery have a pleasing setting within a grove of trees. Turn left onto Wembley Road.

DR. ROBERT BROWN, leader of the Vancouver Island Exploring Expedition of 1864, said of this area in his reports: " . . . in some instances you find beautiful flats stretching along the shore, and dotted with clumps of trees, and intersected by sloughs of the sea, so as to be partially overflowed during high tides, but as often elevated flats or downs, or waht are known in the north of Scotland as "links". I may especially note the beautiful tract extending from the Rio de Grullas (River of

Cranes — Englishman River) of the Spaniards, to past Quall-e-hum (Qualicum) River, and capable of affording good pasturage for thousands of cattle."

Mr. & Mrs. Kinkade by the doorway of their square timber home.

5.0 FRENCH CREEK: A year after the first settler, John Hirst, chose the Parksville site for his homestead in 1874, a Frenchman with the strange name of Harry de Greek is believed to have come to this area, and it is assumed that French Creek received its name from him.

The Creek is eleven miles long with a light run of steelhead in spring and fall. Mid-January to end of February offers good fly fishing for coho salmon. Rainbow, Kamloops and cutthroat trout average one to eight pounds.

A quarter-mile down the side road will be found a Government boat basin where you can rent a boat and tackle to try your luck for Coho salmon usually running mid-August to mid-October.

6.8 EAGLECREST: Some of the best specimens of early log structures can be seen in the houses, barns and other buildings on this property. Turn east on the road to the golf course.

8.7 QUALICUM BEACH, population 2884, probably holds the honour of being the most popular ocean strand on the Island. Thousands come here every summer to enjoy the excellent swimming and sun-bathing and to relax in the holiday atmosphere. The "Village" is one-half mile away where will be found the various shops that serve the community.

A variety of beach cottages, motels, and hotels are available in the area, plus many commercial and government tenting and trailer camps. For the golfer there is a popular course with a sweeping view of the Straits.

10.7 KINKADE ROAD: Take a short drive down this road to the flat delta of the Little Qualicum River. Here in 1884 Thomas Kinkade tied up his eight-ton sloop, the "Sally", and lived on it with his family for nearly a year while he built a home of hand-hewn timbers. He purchased 160 of these acres and went to work to reclaim the tide and river-inundated flats. With a wheelbarrow and shovel he built two dykes which still stand today. The original home and barn can be seen from the road.

The Kinkades found the remains of a large stockade and many skeletons on the site. Visiting Indians told them small-pox had killed many of the dwellers and the survivors had set fire to the village when they fled.

Now the property of the Federal Government, under the care of Environment Canada and designated a National Wildlife Area. It is to be hoped that in due course, funds will be found that will enable the authorities to make the area accessible to the public under proper control and conditions. An arrangement that will please the hearts of visiting bird watchers when one realizes that the staff on site have sighted a list of 215 bird species.

11.2 LITTLE QUALICUM RIVER: Late winter, early spring and the fall months are the best periods to fish this river. It is one of the best year-round fishing streams on the Island. The river entrance was a favourite place for early Indians to set their salmon traps of cedar stakes and willow branches. Here they camped in early fall and caught and smoked thousands of fish.

A quiet retreat.

17.2 HORNE LAKE JUNCTION: Approximately five miles west of the Island highway is Horne Lake. It is five miles long by one mile wide, and its best season is May to October for rainbow, Kamloops, and cutthroat trout. The road passes near Spider Lake which has probably the best black bass fishing on the Island. Try for them from July to October.

Who was the first white man to cross the Island to the Alberni Inlet? How did he go? Evidently some of the east coast Indians were quite familiar with a route used to cross the mountains, so it was to be expected that some trader would investigate it. Adam Horne, a giant of a man, worked for the Hudson's Bay Company at Fort Nanaimo and an entry in the Fort Journal dated Saturday, May 10th, 1856 gives this information: "Tom Ouatomy left here on an expedition across the Island, accompanied by three Indians and one Indian woman. Mr. Horne also left with him (and with) instructions not to proceed farther than the high mountains beyond the large lake in the interior, but if the interior tribes be peaceable he may proceed to Alberni Canal." The "large lake" was thereafter known as Horne Lake.

Attempts are being made to have a road built that would follow this "Route of the Pioneers", as it is known. This would open up a large area to the traveller, including the famous Euclataw caves.

17.5 BIG QUALICUM FISHERIES PROJECT: Salmon entering British Columbia's coastal streams in the fall to spawn have had to overcome tremendous odds to reach this final stage of their life cycle. Of 3,000 eggs deposited in the gravel by spawning salmon, 300 survive and develop into sea-going fry. From these only four will return as spawning adults three or four years later.

In an attempt to increase their chances of survival, the Federal Department of Fisheries and Oceans, conducts a salmon production program on the Big Qualicum river. The project is unique and claims to represent the first environmental control program for salmon propogation in the world. The public is welcome to view the project. You will be pleasantly surprised at what you will find just one-half mile up the road.

101

18.0 QUALICUM CAMPSITE is located on sixty acres with a safe beach and play area. As well as the usual amenities, there is a salmon barbecue pit. The beach and campgrounds are maintained and operated by the Qualicum Indian Band. There are 40 campsites and a number of picnic tables.

18.5 QUALICUM BAY consists of a collection of motels, trailer and tent parks, and waterfront homes fronting on the beach.

21.3 BOWSER: A small community on bench-land overlooking the ocean, named for a former premier of the province.
"The only canine bartender in the world!" was the statement made in Ripley's Believe It Or Not when describing "Mike", who was trained by Bowser Hotel owners Mr. and Mrs. Charles Winfield to carry a bottle of beer in his mouth to their customers, bring the money to the bar and return the change. Mike performed this feat for seven years before his death in 1941. The hotel, constructed in 1925, was destroyed by fire in 1969.

24.5 MOUNTAIN VIEW: This is one of the comparatively few places on the main Highway where one can glimpse the

A typical settler's cabin. Note the excellent workmanship with peeled cedar logs and sturdy, cedar shake roof.

high mountains forming the undulating backbone of the Island. Large scale reforestation projects, initiated some thirty years ago by the B.C. Forest Service, have clothed them in a dense stand of Douglas fir.

31.3 FANNY BAY is linked with the hey-day of logging along this coast. Some old camp buildings and the remains of wharves and pilings can still be seen. The small Fanny Bay Hotel built in the early thirties is the only hold-over of these earlier boom-days.

31.5 DENMAN AND HORNBY ISLANDS: Denman shows as a long low island with its timberlands cut by the smooth green swaths of farms. Hornby Island is hidden behind the mass of the former. Both places depend on farming, logging and tourist activities. The nearby ferry runs to Denman where you will find Fillongley Park with 10 campsites and 12 picnic sites. There are many access points to the shoreline around the island. On the way to Gravelly Bay and the Hornby Island ferry, you will pass by many of the Island's pleasant farms.

While there are no public campgrounds on Hornby, you will find private campsites as well as a number of bed & breakfast facilities. Whaling Station Bay and Tribune Bay have good sandy beaches and picnic tables. Helliwell Provincial Park has picnic tables plus nature trails where you can discover the unspoiled beauties of these islands. Petroglyphs and unique geolocal rock formations can be found on Hornby's shoreline.

Many of the Islanders are involved in a variety of crafts, notably weaving and pottery. During the summer months their work is on display in the local library. The Islands are worth a visit if only for a few hours.

It is a 10 minute ferry ride to Denman and a 10 minute run from Denman to Hornby.

35.2 BAYNES SOUND: An excellent picnic and rest area with a panoramic view of the Strait of Georgia, Denman Island, massive Texada Island in the distance and the mainland mountains beyond. Oyster farming is practiced in these waters and some of the harvest is sold in nearby shops and restaurants.

37.5 UNION BAY: This community took its name from the Union Coal Mining Company that started the mines at nearby Cumberland. Twelve miles of track were laid between the mines and the dock facilities, built in 1889. A steady stream of ships came to this port to fill bunkers for their own boilers and to load coal for various parts of the world. Some traces of this former activity can still be seen today, including moun-

Coal and coke facilities at Union Bay during its heyday.

tains of waste coal, providing mute testimony to the grand scale of the operations.

42.3 TRENT RIVER: Discovery of coal in 1869 resulted in "diggings" along Trent and Coal Creeks into the foothills, with little mining results, until the Dunsmuir interest of Wellington became interested.

43.0 ROYSTON is a fine residential community on slopes overlooking Comox Harbour.

You can continue on to Courtenay or go through Cumberland to Kin Park and boat launching facilities on Comox Lake. By boat you can take a short water trip to another picnic site, halfway up the lake at Pierce Point, provided by the Crown Zellerbach

Logging Company. Comox Lake is eight miles long and one mile wide and offers cutthroat, Dolly Varden, and Kokanee, as well as salmon fishing during summer and fall. Rowboats and horses are available.

CUMBERLAND: Population 1,720. Four miles west of Royston, the town originally known as Union, was renamed by Robert Dunsmuir after the County of Cumberland in England, home of many of the miners in the area.

The occurrence of coal in this region had been noted as early as the 1850s by J.W. McKay of the Hudson's Bay Company. Again, in 1864, Dr. Robert Brown of the Vancouver Island Exploring Expedition discovered coal seams on Brown's River north of Comox Lake. Then in 1869 an Indian visiting at Nanaimo told some coal miners that he know where there was

One of the largest on the continent, Cumberland's Chinatown slowly disappeared after the closing of the mines.

more of the "black stone". They left Nanaimo to investigate and at the end of their journey the Indian showed the excited men seams of coal beside the edge of Coal Creek near the Cumberland of today.

The group formed the Union Coal Mining Company and commenced operations. The coal had to be brought to tidewater and attempts were made to arrange a rail line to Royston but before agreements could be made the miners ran out of money.

This was the cue for Dunsmuir at Wellington to buy the claims for his rapidly expanding empire. The first project was to cut a road from Royston to Cumberland, much of it along the route as it is today. He then tried to negotiate for a rail terminal at Comox Harbour in Royston, but when confronted with exorbitant prices he moved south and founded Union Bay in 1889.

As many as seven producing mines were opened, some not as productive as others, but Number Four proved to be a bonanza, continuing to pour out coal for almost fifty years before its closure in the late 1930s. Before the turn of the century one mine alone was yielding 25,000 tons a day. As a result Comox Coal became well known throughout the northwest.

By 1955 mining ended except for a few small workings and all work ceased by 1967, ending eighty years of coal mining activity on Vancouver Island.

46.0 COMOX VALLEY TOURIST BUREAU and Chamber of Commerce: This well-run service is one mile from the centre of Courtenay. The staff will advise you on the many attractions and activities to be found in the valley. The valley is one of the major cultural centres of the Island hosting an annual Youth Music Centre and craft fairs.

BYPASS: for those in a hurry to get to Comox or further north. Continue straight ahead to reach the centre of Courtenay.

47.0 COURTENAY: Population 8992 and Comox 6697 are sister communities whose early histories are bound together. Courtenay was named after Rear Admiral George William Courtenay, Captain of the "H.M.S. Constance" which plied the coast from 1846 to 1849. Komuckway, meaning "plenty" or "abundance" was the name of an early Indian tribe that lived in the area. Through progressive white man's spelling, Komuckway became Komoux then Comox.

The year was 1862 when the first white settlers came to the Comox Valley, many of them from New Zealand who had come to British Columbia lured by the thoughts of gold but gave up the idea in favour of farming and fishing. Their choice was wise

106

for in 1860 the survey ship "H.M.S. Plumper" reported: ". . . the extent and beauty of what we saw quite surprised us, and we agreed that this was the most promising spot for an agriculture settlement we have yet seen on the Island."

1876 saw the building of the wharf at Comox and the establishment of a Navy Training Base on the spit. At the same time, the Hudson's Bay Company opened a trading post. The Courtenay Hotel was built in the late 1880s and is still in use today—it was in the area of this hotel that the early settlement developed. Finally, in 1890 a new townsite was begun on the west side of the river. With the arrival of the E & N Railway in 1914, the produce and resources of the valley found their way to many markets.

COURTENAY MUSEUM has recently been relocated in a massive log building built in 1928 by the Native Sons organization. This former community centre now houses new displays including an Indian longhouse reconstruction, collections of early Chinese crafts, and a complete Chinese store with precious Chinese handicrafts and instruments. A fine community project worth your visit. Open daily in the summer.

While this is a centre for extensive farming, logging and some commercial fishing, Courtenay and Comox have, as well, much to offer for the visitor: extensive facilities both private and public are available for fishing, camping, swimming, exploring, hiking and golf, while nearby Forbidden Plateau and Mount Washington are two of British Columbia's major skiing facilities.

FORBIDDEN PLATEAU: This unusual name derives from a legend of the Comox Indians. It was told how once, when Cowichan warriors threatened to attack the village, the Comox men sent their womenfolk and children up into this mountainous highland, believing the region to be a safe hiding place with ample fish and game. But when the Cowichan were repelled and the Comox defenders sought their families, not a trace was ever found near the lakes nor in the forests. They feared hairy giants had cast everyone over the cliffs of what is now known as Cruickshank Canyon. The plateau became taboo and was given a title of "Hiyu Cultus Illahe", (Plenty Bad Place) which white explorers in the 1920s expressed by the present name.

An early Indian village near Comox.

Today Forbidden Plateau is an all-season mountain recreational area, especially for skiers, hikers, mountaineers, and the trout fisherman seeking a challenge off the beaten track. Some trails have been developed, but if you are not accompanied by someone familiar with the area, you should check with the Courtenay Recreation Association or sport shops about current hiking or skiing conditions.

Those who venture westward through the sub-alpine scenery, and on into the higher mountain country, will be rewarded with fine panoramas by ascending the summit areas of Mt. Becher (4,538 feet, a day hike) or Mt. Albert Edward (6,868 feet, a two-day trip). At any time of year, it is worth driving up the eleven miles for an unforgettable view of the Strait of Georgia and the imposing Coast Mountain Range on the mainland. It would be wise, however, to check locally as to the road conditions, winter or summer. The road crosses Brown's River which meanders over sun-warmed rocks forming delightful small waterfalls and bath-sized pools. Fun swimming for all ages.

COMOX is the site of a large air force and rescue station, and a commercial airport nearby is a terminal for flights to the mainland and northern Island points. Comox is also the terminus of the B.C. Ferry service to Powell River on the mainland.

A drive through Comox and on to Cape Lazo is rewarding, for at the Cape you will find swimming and picnic facilities while you enjoy an unsurpassed view of the Strait of Georgia. Be sure to return from Comox by way of Glacier Drive, to catch the tremendous view of the valley and the Comox Glacier nestled in the mountain backbone of Vancouver Island (see the frontispiece photograph).

The sun highlights the Mt. Becher approach to Forbidden Plateau. This region offers excellent cross-country skiing during winter.

A view from Miracle Beach of the Coast Mountains.

Courtenay to Campbell River

As late as the 1890s there was but a foot trail leading northward from the Comox Valley. It was a twelve-hour hike from Courtenay to the Campbell River area, with streams and rivers to cross on fallen trees, but by 1904 a rough wagon road was in use.

0.0 COURTENAY: Commence mileages at corner of Cliffe Avenue and 5th Street. Turn east and proceed across Courtenay River. See map 6 and 7.

0.3 JUNCTION TO COMOX: A three mile drive will bring you to the centre of Comox. Here is a view of the harbour and spit westward to Royston and the main Island highway. Comox has a nine-hole golf course and attractive parks including picnic areas and tennis courts.

0.5 JUNCTION TO POWELL RIVER FERRY: It is five miles to the ferry terminal. Drive a short distance up this road to enjoy a splendid panoramic view of the valley and the Comox glacier in the mountains beyond. An excellent photograph of this scene faces our title page.

0.7 TO FORBIDDEN PLATEAU AND BROWN'S RIVER: Check locally re the road conditions in winter. See page 108.

0.9 PIONEER CHURCH: Constructed in 1873 and preceded

111

by a log church built on the site in 1862, this well-preserved building invokes many memories for the older residents of the valley.

3.3 SUNNYDALE GOLF AND COUNTRY CLUB is an attractive nine-hole course which visitors are welcome to use.

7.5 MERVILLE: The Provincial Land Settlement Board chose this area for a soldier settlement scheme after the 1914-18 war. Originally it was a forest wilderness covered in great stands of fir and cedar. Around the turn of the century it was logged by wasteful large-scale operations that swept virgin timber from thousands of acres of benchland and mountain slope. The community was started in 1919 with considerable difficulty for the land was covered with huge stumps, any one of which would take a week's labour to remove.

11.0 BLACK CREEK: This region of the Island remained a virtual wilderness for several decades after settlers arrived in Courtenay, with only two settlers between Black Creek and Campbell River. Many of the later settlers to this area were Mennonite Brethren and their descendants are still found locally.

13.7 MIRACLE BEACH: This provincial park and campground has 178 campsites, 73 picnic sites, and an interesting nature house, plus staff for lectures and trail walks. This is one of the better parks in which to learn of the Island's natural beauties.

14.6 SARATOGA BEACH is an area of resorts fronting on a beautiful sandy beach. There is no public camping but there is access to the beach for swimming.

14.9 OYSTER RIVER is a popular river for fly fishermen. Rainbow and cutthroat trout up to 16 inches are frequently taken on this 15-mile stream.

15.8 RESEARCH FARM: This 1500-acre farm is operated by the University of British Columbia for faculty and students to conduct research and gain experience in the breeding and feeding of dairy cattle. The 350-head ranks as one of Vancouver Island's largest dairy herds. The public is welcome to stop and visit.

17. OYSTER BAY PICNIC SITE: An excellent stop for viewing the northern end of the Strait of Georgia.

22.6 HISTORICAL STOP OF INTEREST: As you view the southern entrance to Discovery Passage and contemplate Captain Vancouver taking his Royal Navy sloop "Discovery" into this narrow, tide-ripped channel in 1792, consider as well the Euclataws, a southern band of Kwakiutl Indians, who occupied the strategic site at Cape Mudge on Quadra Island across the channel.

From their vantage point overlooking these dangerous narrows, they raided or extracted toll from Indian and white trading parties travelling to and from Fort Victoria. Travellers came to fear "the hole of death" where they faced the double threat of very treacherous winds, tides and whirlpools, as well as the maurading Euclataws. Only the ominous presence of the colonial gunboat finally curbed this piracy.

23.1 WILLOWS POINT: A small community five miles south of Campbell River.

24.9 A GLACIAL ERRATIC: This "calling card" of a huge glacier was carried intact down out of the mountains by the river of ice and left stranded several thousand years ago.

QUADRA ISLAND: The traveller approaching Campbell River from the south, sees ahead the imposing bluffs of Cape Mudge on Quadra Island. Rising over 200 feet, they have a commanding view south, of the Strait of Georgia. The Cape was named for Lieut. Zachary Mudge, who in 1792 climbed it to take observations for the ship "Discovery". The Cape was equipped with a lighthouse in 1898 to guide ships into the narrow entrance of Discovery Passage.

The Island, largest of the "Discovery Group", has a population of approximately 1,200. About 20 miles long, it is reached by a 10-minute ferry ride from Campbell River and merits a visit.

It is an ideal area to hike, fish, picnic, gather oysters and clams, or do some beachcombing. There is a provincial park at Rebecca Spit with 32 campsites, 9 picnic sites and a boat ramp with mooring facilities. In the same area the Cape Mudge Indian Band operates an excellent campground. There are other commercial facilities available to make your stay enjoyable.

28.0 CAMPBELL RIVER: On the eastern shore of Vancouver Island where the Campbell flows into the turbulent waters of Discovery Passage, stands the town famous for the large trees in the surrounding forests and the record salmon that are caught in the nearby waters.

Only five settlers lived in the area of Campbell River in 1900, but with the fast developing interest in lumbering and commercial fishing, settlement was inevitable. The building of a hotel in 1904, followed by other commercial establishments, saw the beginning of what has developed steadily through the years to become today's modern community.

Geographically, Campbell River is about half way up-island from Victoria, and was for many years the "end of the road". But with the development of hydroelectric power at Elk Falls in the 40s; the construction of a pulp and paper mill at nearby Duncan Bay in the 50s; with the opening of a network of roads in the northern half of the Island; plus the building of a pulp mill at Gold River on the west coast, Campbell River has seen steady economic growth and has become the major distribution centre for the northern half of the Island. The almost unlimited scope for ocean and fresh water sport fishing, camping, hiking, and general outdoor enjoyment has made the area a mecca for holidayers.

Famous are the big Chinook salmon that run 60 to 70 pounds or better. Known as Springs by the commercial fisherman and Tyee (when over 30 pounds) by the sport fisherman, they are the largest of the salmon species. The Tyee Club of Campbell River was formed in 1925. It offers membership to anyone for catching a Tyee using club regulation tackle. Many proud fishermen throughout the world have become members. As in other areas of the Island, complete fishing services, including guides, boats and tackle are available if you wish to try for a Tyee. There are also canning and smoking facilities for taking your catch home.

Highlight of the year in Campbell River is the annual Salmon Festival in July, which includes a parade, water sports, street dancing, fishing derby, war canoe races, and much more. The tourist bureau should be your first stop for local information, and be sure to visit the excellent local museum.

Campbell River to Kelsey Bay

A road link to the north was slow in coming. From the early 1900s, election promises and the pleading of settlers had failed to bring a much needed road north to Kelsey Bay. It took World War II and the threat of a possible invasion from the north down Johnstone Strait to force the government into action in the early 1940s.

0.0 CAMPBELL RIVER TOURIST INFORMATION CENTRE Highway 19. Proceed north.

1.4 JUNCTION: Turn right and continue on Highway 19.

1.6 CAMPBELL RIVER BRIDGE: The Campbell River is three miles long with good grilse and steelhead fishing. This river attracts fishermen from all over the world who come here seeking the famous Tyee salmon.

3.7 ELK FALLS PULP AND PAPER MILL is one of the most modern forest products manufacturing plants in Canada, representing an investment of $500 million. Over 1300 people are employed here and the products are found in homes throughout the world. Tours of the plant are available, but before doing so it is recommended that you drive a short distance farther to a viewpoint overlooking the site:

3.9 VIEWPOINT: From here on Duncan Bay the overall setting of the mill can be observed.

The Ripple Rock blast.

7.7 HISTORICAL STOP OF INTEREST: Ripple Rock achieved world-wide attention at 9:31 a.m., on April 5th, 1958, when, at the push of a button, one of the largest non-atomic explosions in the history of man literally blew it "sky-high".

Ever since 1792 when the first European, Capt. George Vancouver, carefully brought his sailing ship "Discovery" through this perilously narrow passage, a twin-headed rock in the centre of the channel had claimed its toll of lives. Over twenty major shipwrecks and over a hundred minor ones have been attributed to it; the loss of life since 1875 is reported to be 114 persons.

Ripple Rock had two summits, one being less than ten feet underwater at low tide, the other less than twenty feet. Each year the Rock, with its swirling eddies and whirlpools, forced ships to wait until the tide was high, yet it was an essential channel of the "Inside Passage" to Prince Rupert and Alaska.

To remove this "sailor's nightmare", it was decided to drill a shaft on Maude Island and then run out beneath the sea-bed to a point below the rock. A "raise" would be made to reach close under the twin peaks, where enough explosive would be stored to blow off the top of the rock. This plan was culminated, after 2½ years' work and an expenditure of $3,100,000, in the plugging of the tunnels and "coyote holes" honeycombing the top of Ripple Rock with high power explosive. Enough explosive to fill 34 box-cars made the long trip through the various shafts and tunnels to its brief resting place, only a few feet beneath the ocean's surface.

As tension mounted before the blast, there were predictions of tidal waves and building collapses and other fearful disturbances. The town of Campbell River turned off public services and "battened down the hatches". Then, precisely on schedule and in full view of batteries of TV cameras flashing the spectacle to the world, the surface of Seymour Narrows erupted in an awesome billow of hurtling rock and frothing water. It was over in seconds except for a cloudy mist that spread across the channel. In the estimated 700,000 tons of rock and water shredded by the blast, Ripple Rock "blew its top" leaving a clearance now of 47 feet and safe passage for ships.

Despite the immensity of the explosion there wasn't a single broken window, overturned boat, or collapsed wharf.

11:45 PM Saturday, June 30, 1984, the 17,500 ton cruise ship Sundancer hit a rock at Maude Island at the entrance to Seymour Narrows. It managed to limp into the dock at the Elk Falls Mill, where it settled into the mud. Fortunately, no loss of life.

20.5 ROBERTS LAKE is just over a mile long, lying at the foot of Menzies Mountain (4,603 feet). Trolling can yield catches of trout to three pounds and cabins and boats are available. There are many good locations for picnicking and swimming.

23.9 AMOR DE COSMOS CREEK: William Alexander Smith of Nova Scotia, by an act of the California Legislature, changed his name to Amor de Cosmos, meaning "Lover of the Universe". He became the second premier of the province 1872-1874. See page 40.

39.3 SALMON RIVER: This major river is 46 miles long and flows north to Kelsey Bay. This is a good steelhead river and some of the Island's largest have been caught in it. Salmon and trout can be taken at its mouth.

40.4 JUNCTION: East to Sayward & Kelsey Bay, north to Port Hardy. West to the White River store for travel information.

41.2 LINK AND PIN MUSEUM is a fine example of what can be done to preserve historical treasures and make them present-able for everyone's enjoyment and education. Note also the unusual "Cable Cookhouse" next door.

44.4 STONE GATE MEMORIAL: Just before crossing the Salmon River again, you will notice stone gate posts with an inscription on one which reads: "Blessed be they that spare these stones, but cursed be they that remove them." Erected as a memorial of the Golden Wedding Anniversary of John and Jane Armishaw in 1943, they mark the property on which their home once stood. In 1913 the Armishaw family moved to Sayward from the mainland and John Armishaw became the first Justice of the Peace in this area. He also actively crusaded for a road to Campbell River and Cape Scott, and was to see the Campbell River road completed in 1944, one year before his death.

Mrs. Armishaw found the laundry facilities unique, to say the least. The family built a large float at their river landing, with a roof over a stove, tubs, and scrub boards. Rinsing was done in the river; drying and bleaching on the fields.

47.5 SAYWARD, population 464, is a small logging and farming community named for William Sayward, who moved to Vancouver Island in 1858 and engaged in the lumbering business. Mr. H. Otto Sacht in 1902 built a general store. The counter was a single fir "plank" measuring 32 feet long, 32 inches high and two feet thick. An old account book lists the following: eighteen pounds of butter at $4.50; seven dozen eggs at $1.75; two sacks of carrots at $1.50; fifteen pounds of Blue Ribbon Tea at $6.75; one hundred pounds of potatoes at $1.00; twenty pounds of sugar at $1.35, and twelve yards calico at $2.00. The Hastings Logging Company moved into the valley in 1905. Wages amounted to approximately three dollars per day for loggers, board extra.

By 1913 there were almost 100 people in this valley with the only communication to the outside world by boat. This was the year the Government built a pack-trail to Campbell River. The following year there was a land rush based on an election promise of a road. This failed to materialize, but still many fine farms had been established. Today Sayward centres around farming and vast logging operations, and still attracts people with a strong desire to pioneer.

48.0 KELSEY BAY was named for M.W. Kelsey, who with his family was a pioneer in the area in the early 1920s. Prior to 1892 a prosperous Indian village was situated here at the mouth of the Salmon River.

A vast number of private logging roads in this area lead to good lakes and streams for fishing, but use of the roads is strictly by permission and only during specified hours. You should make your enquiries at the MacMillan Bloedel field office for the necessary information.

PORT NEVILLE is on the mainland side of the Strait, about eight miles out of Kelsey Bay. The Daily Colonist of Victoria reported in the issue of June 25, 1925: "Hansom's Lumber Camp at Port Neville is seriously threatened by a huge forest fire. Reports from the scene of the conflagration indicate that the scene of operations is in greater danger." Again on June 28th: "50 men are fighting a losing battle against a forest fire which threatens to drive them to the water at any moment."

119

Newspaper reports indicate that this was a very serious year for the forests, with temperatures soaring into the high nineties; the woods were a tinder box and fires were breaking out throughout the province. The temperature in Victoria was the highest recorded in 51 years—95.1°F.

The Port Neville forest fire, with residents taking to the boats.

Sayward Junction to Port Hardy

THE 76 miles of new highway you are about to travel, was completed in 1979, eliminating the need to travel north from Kelsey Bay by ferry, or over the logging road from Gold River. Built to the highest standards with an easy gradient to the summit which at 1400 feet is the highest point on the Island highway. The sweeping vistas along the Adam and Eve rivers and Nimpkish Lake will long remain in your memory.

0.0 SAYWARD JUNCTION.

5.6 KETA LAKE REST AREA.

12.0 ADAM RIVER.

14.2 ROONEY LAKE: Picnic site and boat launch. For the next few miles you will notice examples of reforestation on both sides of the highway.

18.0 EVE RIVER REST AREA.

34.8 JUNCTION: The right fork goes to Mt. Caen for skiing in the winter and hiking in the summer. Eight miles down the west fork to Schoen Lake Provincial Campground you will find 10 campsites, boat launch and swimming. This road will also take you to Klaklakama Lake (about six miles), where Canadian Forest Products have provided 13 campsites and a boat launch. A further five miles brings you to Vernon Lake with 22 campsites, boat launch and good swimming. This has also been provided by C.F.P.

37.7 HOOMAK LAKE: Picnic and rest area.

41.7 WOSS: Headquarters of Canadian Forest Products Englewood Logging Division. At the office you can procure a map of the area and any further information you may need. There is a restaurant and gas station in the village. Nearby Woss Lake has 15 campsites, picnic tables and toilets.

44.5 REST AREA.

54.1 JUNCTION: Atluck Lake with a boat launching ramp but no camping facilities, is seven miles west. Bonanza Lake with boat launching and camping is about the same distance east.

NIMPKISH VALLEY: For many centuries, the Nimpkish River and lake system was a major travel route for Indians moving across Vancouver Island from their villages near the mouth of the river on the east coast to Muchalat Inlet on the west. Travelling in their dugout canoes along these waterways, it was "a journey of four days across the land to Nootka Inlet" as was explained to Captain Vancouver when he visited the region in 1792.

Today, the Nimpkish Valley is honeycombed with close to 300 miles of logging roads and one of the largest, logging railroad networks on the continent. Along the seventy five miles of "mainline" trackage, much of which is visible as one travels north along the lake, logs are hauled to the dumping grounds at Beaver Cove, made up into rafts, and then towed two hundred miles to the company's manufacturing plants on the mainland.

76.0 JUNCTION: Beaver and Telegraph Coves are eight miles to the right. It is worth a trip to Telegraph Cove. There you will find a viewing area where you can watch the booming operations in the waters below. Beaver Cove was the terminus of a ferry route from Kelsey Bay and was in operation until the new

Beaver Cove booming grounds.

road was opened in 1979. Turn left for Port McNeill and Port Hardy.

9.0 NIMPKISH RIVER CROSSING: The mouth of the river is a short distance downstream from the bridge. It was here that Captain Vancouver arrived at 10:00 p.m. July 19th, 1792, and anchored his vessel, the "Discovery". His account of his visit follows: "The next morning showed the village in our neighbourhood to be large; and, from the number of our visitors, it appears to be very populous. These brought us the skins of the sea-otter, of an excellent quality, in great abundance, which we bartered for sheet copper, and blue cloth; those articles being in the highest estimation amongst them. The Ty-eie or chief of the village, paid us an early visit, and received from me some presents which highly delighted him. I understood his name to be Cheslakees."

123

CHESLAKEES CAMPSITE: Turn left before crossing the bridge—the campsite is a short distance up-river. Canadian Forest Products Ltd. created this facility of 22 units, including picnic tables and restrooms. Tyee and coho salmon can be caught at the mouth of the river during August and September, cutthroat and Dolly Varden from May to October.

84.0 PORT McNEILL with a population of 2474 is two miles down the road. Named after Captain William McNeill, in employ of the Hudson's Bay Company and one-time master of the Company's famous trading vessel "Beaver". The Port serves as a distribution and services centre for much of the area. B.C. Ferries provide a regular service from here to Alert Bay on Cormorant Island and Sointula on Malcolm Island.

ALERT BAY population 760, is often called "The Crossroads of the North", for much of the water traffic north or southbound stops here to re-fuel, provision, and exchange news of other settlements throughout the Inside Passage.

This Indian village is a fascinating mixture of the past and present. Modern as most communities, it is also the heart of the Kwakiutl Indian Nation, for it was here the Indians gathered from surrounding areas during the salmon fishing season, although they made no permanent settlement on Cormorant Island until about 1870.

Ships on tour to northern ports of British Columbia and Alaska make Alert Bay a stop in summer to allow their passengers time to visit the museum, admire the totems and watch native ceremonies and dances performed at the community house.

A most interesting place to visit for a day. The B.C. Ferry makes the round trip to Alert Bay and Sointula every two hours, giving you ample time to enjoy the visit before returning. You will not be disappointed.

SOINTULA on Malcolm Island was settled in 1902 by a group of Finnish immigrants as an attempt at communal living. Success perhaps could have been achieved, but for a number of difficulties that arose which served to break up the community. Logging, fishing, and farming form the way of life for the families that remain.

Kwakiutl totem poles, like these at Alert Bay, were designed by the carver to represent spiritual or personal conditions that surrounded him or his family. On the left the mythical thunderbird glowers over a bear embracing a human figure. The figure at right is adorned with what represents a copper breastplate, which was a symbol of great wealth.

89.8 CLUXEWE BEACH CAMPGROUND: Operated by the Fort Rupert Indian Band, they provide 35 campsites, picnic area, and running water. A great place to camp and do some beachcombing.

91.7 LOOKOUT: Pull off the road here where you can absorb the expansive view of Queen Charlotte Strait and the solemn beauty of the Coast Range mountains on the mainland. Mount Waddington at 13,260 feet, is the second highest summit in the province and forms the "master-stroke" in this panorama. Malcolm Island, separated from Vancouver Island by Broughton Strait, lies in the foreground. Picnic tables and toilets are available.

96.4 PORT ALICE JUNCTION: The following indented mileage figures and descriptions are for travelling to Port Alice, otherwise continue to the junction at mile 108.4

0.2 BEAVER LAKE PARK: The Rayonier Company has built this picnic site, installed tables, fire pits, and toilets. The lake water is warm if you would like to swim.

8.5 MARBLE RIVER originates at Alice Lake, a short distance up-stream, and flows for six miles to Rupert Inlet. It is known for good trout fishing year round, a summer run of steelhead, and a winter run of steelhead from November to March, with December being the best month. This is a fast, dangerous river and extreme caution must be exercised in any exploration of it.

MARBLE RIVER CAMPGROUND is an excellent park created by the Rayonier Company. A boat launching ramp for access to Alice Lake has been provided, plus picnic tables, toilets and 33 campsites.

8.7 ALICE LAKE is eight miles long and offers trout fishing throughout the season. An excellent lake for boating and there is a campsite with 10 pads plus a sandy beach.

12.0 LARIE LAKE: Good fishing in this small body of water. For the next couple of miles Alice Lake can be seen far below.

17.6 JEUNE LANDING: Headquarters for the Rayonier Company's logging division on the shores of Neroutsos Inlet.

19.0 PORT ALICE, population 1668. In 1964 construction began of a new townsite here at Rumble Beach, and the phasing out of the old town at the millsite. On June 16, 1965, the new Port Alice became British Columbia's first "instant

These 20 foot lower jaw-bones of a blue whale are on display at Coal Harbour. The blue is the largest animal in the world and may grow to 95 feet and weigh 150 tons.

municipality". This delightful and well-planned modern community, with its homes, shopping centre, schools, hotel and community centre blends into the forest background, overlooking the inlet and the mountains beyond.

23.0 MILLSITE: August 1918, saw the first pulp produced at Port Alice. A townsite of 50 homes, a hotel and a rooming house was also provided. The mill ownership changed a number of times until 1954 when Rayonier of Canada acquired control. Port Alice, Alice Lake and Victoria Lake were named after members of the Whalen family, the original builders of the pulp mill.

25.0 VICTORIA LAKE is ten miles long. There is good trout fishing for most of the year, either fly or trolling. There is a boat launching ramp at the end of the road.

108.4 JUNCTION: Left to Port Hardy, right to Beaver Harbour. It is three miles to the Beaver Harbour section of the Port Hardy municipality.

HISTORICAL STOP OF INTEREST: In Port Hardy Centennial Park, at Beaver Harbour, the story of Fort Rupert is told. Established by the Hudson's Bay Company in 1849 to protect and work the coal deposits found there, it became a home for the miners and a trading post to which the Indians brought furs and salmon. This, then, became the only white settlement outside of Victoria. It was here that Robert Dunsmuir first lived as a coal miner when he came to the Island from Scotland in 1851. The stockade was destroyed by fire in 1889, and in the years to follow, the bastions and living quarters, decaying with age, were torn down. Only the stone fireplace and chimney remain.

A picnic site and sandy beach has been provided in the park. The nearby airport serves this north end of the Island with daily flights to the mainland and other Island points.

110.3 BEAR COVE ROAD to British Columbia Ferries terminal.

111.0 COAL HARBOUR ROAD: A Royal Canadian Airforce station during the war, the hangers and other buildings were converted to a whaling station in the early '50s but now closed.

The giant Utah Copper Mine nearby, one of the world's largest open pit mines, is a sight to behold. From mid-May to the end of August, tours can be arranged by phone from Port Hardy.

QUATSE RIVER PARK has been provided by the Mt. Waddington Regional District and has 44 campsites, picnic tables, restrooms and swimming and fishing in the river.

112.0 PORT HARDY, population 5075 plus, is the largest centre on northern Vancouver Island with extensive service and distribution facilities. No longer referred to as an area of "shattered dreams", it continues to be a fast growing community with new subdivisions, schools and businesses created during the past few years. Much of the impetus has come from the nearby Utah mine which has the largest known deposit of copper in the world.

With the opening of nearby Fort Rupert in 1849, settlement of this area was inevitable. By 1918 there were 22 families and regular service had been instituted by both the Canadian Pacific and Union Steamship Companies. This was the year that saw telephone connections made, but still there were only limited local roads.

Primary activities were logging and fishing. Some farming had been attempted, but many abandoned it on account of the difficulty of clearing land and the lack of roads. By 1929, the population had risen to 142.

The whole area covered by this chapter, abounds in things to do and see. The communities of Alert Bay, Port McNeill, Port Hardy, the logging companies and the Mt. Waddington Regional District, publish information, guides and maps to acquaint you with enough to whet your appetite and curiosity and encourage an extended stay. Loggers Sports Days, Fishing Derby, Fall Fairs, Sea Festivals, Museums, crafts, fishing, hiking and camping, there is something. to interest everyone and sampling the northern hospitality will send you away glad you came and planning to return.

HOLBERG: Thirty miles of gravel road to this community at the head of Holberg Inlet. Together with the nearby San Josef radar base, it is the most northwestern point on the Island that can be reached by automobile.

In 1896, Danish settlers from Minnesota, came to the Cape Scott area to settle and farm. They built homes, dyked, cleared, cultivated the land, and successfully raised cattle, but weather and lack of access to markets seriously hampered their efforts. As a result some left for areas farther south, while a few families started a new settlement at the head of the inlet, naming it and the community Holberg, after a favourite figure found in Danish literature. While the road to Port Hardy, built in 1896, did help, life continued to present hardships difficult to endure. By 1916 only three families were left.

1942 saw the establishment of a floating logging camp in the inlet. It became the largest floating town in the world—over a quarter-mile long, with homes for families complete with electricity, hot and cold water, and gardens. All the services of a conventional town were provided: fire hall, machine shop, pool

Floating logging camps are still used in remote inlets around the Island.

hall, store, bunkhouse and dining room for single men, and a community hall for basketball, dances and movies.

In use until 1956, it was then decided to build a new town on shore, and by 1972 the town had grown, providing homes for 90 families and quarters for 200 single men. 1950 saw construction start on the nearby R.C.A.F. radar site, the westernmost station of the Pine Tree Line system. Manned by Air Force and civilian personnel, it has often been able to "checkout" aircraft in trouble before they ended up lost at sea or on a mountainside.

Georgie, Kains, and Nahwitti Lakes, on the way to Holberg, are reported to offer good fishing and the salmon fishing at Winter harbour is worth a try.

WINTER HARBOUR, 15 miles south of Holberg, is primarily a port for commercial fishermen. The Mt. Waddington Regional District has provided the Kwasksista Campground with seven campsites, picnic tables, running water, and a boat launching ramp.

CAPE SCOTT: The name was given to this northernmost point of Vancouver Island in 1786 by James Strange, who was a fur trader with his partner David Scott.

Wide open to the fury of the Pacific Ocean, it has taken a grim toll of ships and men over the years. A land of rugged shoreline, beautiful sandy beaches, lakes and rivers, it is one of the rainiest areas of the continent, sometimes receiving as much as 200 inches a year.

Tumble-down buildings and rotting equipment can still be seen as mute evidence of early attempts to farm the area. The primitive roads built by the settlers have been all but obliterated by nature. Now the only access is by a rough sixteen-mile trail through the heavy bushland from the radar base to the lighthouse on the Cape. This is not a "Sunday hike" and should not be attempted except by very experienced and well-equipped hikers.

A home for elk, deer, bear, cougar, and waterfowl, it is one of the most recent areas to be set aside as a provincial park. Embracing 38,000 acres and 56 miles of coastline, it will invite only those who appreciate and protect the wilderness.

An old view of a farm in the Cape Scott region. The distant driftwood fence was built to reclaim sand for fields.

The magnificent Butchart Gardens offer a fine aesthetic and educational experience. The daytime beauty becomes magically lit at night.

Victoria to Swartz Bay —Saanich Peninsula

H IGHWAY 17 annually funnels hundreds of thousands of ferry passengers and cars to and from Vancouver Island and the mainland via the terminal at Swartz Bay. The fact that its seventeen-mile length can be covered at high speeds is apt to obscure the many attractive side-trips waiting at every inter-section, cut-off and junction.

Those who elect to leave the busy highway and turn on to the quiet roads of the Saanich Peninsula will be well rewarded. Few places provide a better opportunity to combine the pleasures of the countryside with the delights of the ocean shore. You can linger awhile amid peaceful rural surroundings, yet will always be within a few minutes of attractive sea vistas, shoreline to walk, or trails to hike.

The fifty miles of shoreline is a pleasant contrast to the charming, rural landscape, dominated by bulb, flower, holly and berry farms interspersed with grazing dairy herds, providing an unhurried, relaxing atmosphere for every holiday.

The mileage figures in brackets are for use by those travelling south from the ferry terminal toward Victoria.

0.0 (17.0) SAANICH MUNICIPAL HALL: The metropolitan area you are entering, comprises Saanich with a population of 80,000, Oak Bay 17,000, Esquimalt 11,000 and Victoria 66,000.

133

0.9 (16.1) McKENZIE AVENUE JUNCTION: Turn west for highway No. 1 to go up-island, see page 73. The University of Victoria is three miles east from here, Cadboro Bay is one mile further east which has a small shopping centre, park, playground and beach.

Christmas Hill can be seen to the east and is the setting of a relatively modern Indian legend. It is said that one Christmas Eve over a century ago, a great raven-like bird swooped in from the Pacific, and, from the Indian village on the Inner Harbour at Fort Victoria, snatched an Indian infant and flew off eastward with the baby in its talons. After an all night search by the tribe, fur traders and settlers, the child was found, safe and laughing, among the trees on the summit of this hill.

There is a proposal to reserve Christmas Hill as an ecological teaching area. Only here, in all the metropolitan area, are lupins to be found growing wild and in profusion.

Birdwatchers should be alert for sightings of skylarks throughout the Saanich Peninsula where they are attracted by the vegetable and daffodil farms. Southern Vancouver Island is the only region in North America where this melodious songbird has been successfully introduced. See page 30.

SWAN LAKE: Turn east one block on McKenzie to Rainbow then south on Ralph Street to the Swan Lake Nature Sanctuary. It is well worth a visit to this natural unstructured open space with a nature interpretation centre and walking trail around the lake.

2.8 (13.3) JUNCTION TO HIGHWAY 17 (WEST SAANICH ROAD), MOUNT DOUGLAS PARK AND CORDOVA BAY: Bear right to reach this junction then east three miles to Cordova Bay where you will find a beach access and picnic site. Mount Douglas Park two miles from this junction, provides a fine view of the whole area. There is a short drive to the summit. The nearby beach and picnic/playground are part of the park. Turn west at the junction for access to the Royal Oak Centre and access to Highway 17. The side road running north after the overpass will take you to Beaver Lake Park. Highway 17 a longer but more scenic route to many of the peninsula's popular attractions, including Prospect Lake for swimming,

134

Butchart Gardens, Brentwood Bay village, etc. One of the oldest Anglican churches, St. Michael And All Angels, built in 1883, is a short distance north. See map 2.

HORTICULTURE CENTRE OF THE PACIFIC: Gardeners will find this an interesting place to visit to see the demonstration gardens and learn about garden practices. It is a unique opportunity to observe the varieties of flowers and vegetables and learn about propogation. Less than a mile north on No. 17, turn onto Beaver Road.

THE DOMINION ASTROPHYSICAL OBSERVATORY is located two and a half miles north of the Royal Oak junction on West Saanich Road. Maintained by the National Research Council of Canada, the Observatory is equipped with a 72 inch telescope and is open to the public Monday to Friday from 9:15 AM to 4:30 PM and Saturday evenings 9:00 to 11:00 PM during the months of April to October inclusive.

3.8 (13.2) BEAVER LAKE PARK: Turn west at 4.2 to reach the park (a right turn at 12.8 miles for those coming from the ferry terminal). The park is delightful for families with small children since it offers warm safe swimming, grassy tree-shaded picnic tables, changing rooms and toilet facilities. A very pleasant place to spend a quiet day away from the highway traffic and city noise.

4.8 (12.2) ELK LAKE PARK: Bear left to reach the south end of the lake. Changing rooms and restrooms are provided for swimmers and picnickers. Bass and cutthroat trout can be caught here in early spring.

5.5 (11.5) CUT-OFF: Bear left to reach the north end of Elk Lake. In addition to excellent swimming and picnicking facilities, changing rooms and restrooms, large, grassed playing fields. This tree-shaded oasis is a popular recreation spot for all ages. Canoes and wind surfers can be rented and there is a midget golf course nearby.

5.8 (11.2) JUNCTION: Turn east on Sayward Road to reach the north end of Cordova Bay and the beginning of the "Yellow Dot" scenic route into Victoria. Turn west to reach Brookleigh Road and Elk Lake Park. A boat launching ramp is located about a mile along Brookleigh. One-half mile before the ramp is the beginning of a trail and a twenty minute hike up Bear Hill. You will be rewarded with a wide view of the entire landscape.

7.7 (9.3) CUT-OFF: Bear left to Keating Road and proceed west to reach the world-famous Butchart Gardens. A right turn off Keating Road onto West Saanich Road leads to Brentwood Bay, the Mill Bay Ferry and Tsartlip Campground.

BUTCHART GARDENS, overlooking Tod Inlet, receives top priority on the "must see" list of every visitor to Vancouver Island. This botanical showcase is admired throughout the world for its skillful blending of rare and exotic shrubs, trees and plants mixed with native flora in a colourful and authentic series of formal gardens joined by restful paths, bridges and walkways.

The gardens, which cover 35 of the 130 acres of "Benvenuto", the Butchart estate, began as a hobby by Mr. and Mrs. Robert Butchart who, in 1904, accepted the challenge of beautifying an exhausted limestone quarry that formed part of the "Benvenuto" property. Mr. Butchart pioneered in cement manufacturing in Canada and the tall kilns of the plant he founded can be seen across the inlet at Bamberton. Those with an eye for detail will find many artistic but unobtrusive uses of cement in the construction of the gardens.

The transformation of the bleak quarry into the Sunken Garden of today is proof of the success of the Butcharts' beautification plan. From fifty feet above the quarry floor, the visitor is treated to the illusion of a bowl of color reflected in a mirror-smooth lake and framed by alpine rockeries planted

136

among the steep walls, one of which is bisected by a waterfall. The pool at its base finds its way to the lake by way of a meandering stream on the quarry floor where the visitor can study the great variety of trees and shrubs represented here. As in the formal Italian Garden, the authentic and serene Japanese Garden, and the English Rose Garden, many of the plants were personally collected by the Butcharts during their world travels.

Only a personal tour can do justice to the perfection of detail and the beauty of the creative blending of rock, water, terrain and plants. The addition of a unique, extensive lighting system has added a new dimension to this charming spot. During the summer months, the Gardens sparkle from dusk to closing time in specially-designed illumination of their many features. The cyclical lighting effects on fountains, pools and waterfalls are especially spectacular.

Butchart Gardens are open the year 'round. Meals and light lunches and afternoon tea are served in the restaurants. Flower seeds from the many blooms exhibited in the gardens are available. Adding a touch of hilarity in a musical way, the "Butchart Gardeners" entertain all the family every day Monday through Saturday, prior to the evening stage show.

BRENTWOOD BAY can be reached by driving north on West Saanich Road and turning west on Verdier Avenue. This is a popular take-off spot for salmon fishing excursions into Saanich Inlet, the nearby marinas offer complete boat and tackle rentals as well as guide services.

THE MILL BAY FERRY operates between Brentwood Bay and Mill Bay. The three and a half mile trip takes twenty minutes and delivers the traveller, refreshed from his sea cruise, north of Bamberton and within a short distance from Highway 1, the main north-south route on the Island.

TSARTLIP CAMPGROUND is accessible from West Saanich Road by turning at Stellys Crossroad and driving one half mile

Holly, with its distinctive red berries, being packaged for the continent-wide Christmas market.

west. Operated by the Tsartlip Indian Band, the campground offers a boat launching ramp, 32 campsites suitable for tents or campers.

7.9 (9.1) EAST SAANICH ROAD: Cut-off and proceed north to Saanichton which is the centre of a predominantly agricultural region of fruit, vegetable, flower and dairy farms. The daffodil industry is most impressive; about thirteen million blossoms a year are produced, with shipments made as close as downtown Victoria and as far away as Miami, Florida.

SAANICHTON is the home of British Columbia's oldest agricultural fair. Held annually every Labour Day weekend in September since 1871, it is the oldest fair west of the Great Lakes.

Henry Simpson, a baker from Kent, England and employed by the Hudson's Bay Company, built the Prairie Tavern in

138

Loganberries are a major crop of the Saanich Peninsula. Crops of boysenberries, strawberries and raspberries are also harvested.

Saanichton in 1858. Destroyed by fire, it was replaced by the Prairie Inn in 1893 which is still in use today.

8.3 (8.7) ISLAND VIEW ROAD east ends at a beach overlooking Haro Strait. There is a boat launching ramp at the end of the road.

SAANICH HISTORICAL ARTIFACTS SOCIETY is a volunteer organization with a large collection of farm and household artifacts. Started about 20 years ago, the collection can be seen on the 29 acres of cleared and forested land by turning east on Island View Road then north on Lochside Road. Outstanding features are the many farm machines that have been restored and put into operating condition. Young and old enjoy seeing the 1882 threshing machine in operation driven by a 1907 horse-drawn steam engine.

139

9.8 (7.2) MOUNT NEWTON CROSSROAD: Turn west to go to Saanichton, Brentwood Bay, Butchart Gardens and the Mill Bay ferry. St. Stephens church is down this road about two miles, built in 1862, it is one of the oldest churches in British Columbia.

Saanichton and Brentwood Bay are both small communities with shopping centres, restaurants, post offices, police, service stations and other amenities.

12.6 (4.4) McTAVISH ROAD: Turn west to East Saanich Road then south to find the Federal Government Research Station which is the plant quarantine station for checking fruit trees and grapevines entering Canada. One major research project at the station is the application of solar energy in greenhouses. The public is welcome to visit the station and consult with the staff for information.

On the shores of Patricia Bay, one and a half miles west is the Institue of Ocean Sciences and the Pacific Geoscience Centre. Established in 1978, the Geoscience Centre is engaged in the studies of earth science along Canada's Pacific Rim. The Institute is home to hydrographers and marine scientists whose interests are the coastal waters of British Columbia, the North Pacific Ocean, the western Canadian Arctic and the navigable fresh waters east to the Manitoba border. This complex is well worth a visit, however, tours have to be arranged. Take McTavish Road west to West Saanich Road then north to the Centre.

McTavish Road extends west to West Saanich Road. Coals Bay Park is west off West Saanich Road one block on Ardmore Drive then left on Inverness to the parking lot. It is a few minutes walk to this pleasant and secluded pebble beach.

Turn east off the main highway and travel one mile to reach the Anacortes ferry terminal. The ferry, operated by the Washington State Ferries, travels 36 miles between Sidney and Anacortes through the San Juan Islands in two hours and forty minutes.

Tulista Marine Park, overlooking Bazan Bay, provides picnic tables in a large, grassed playground area.

13.7 (3.3) AIRPORT FLYWAY: The Victoria International airport is reached off McTavish Road.

14.0 (3.0 SIDNEY: Population 7946. Turn east onto the main street, Beacon Avenue, of this delightful town, a community of lovely homes, pleasant shops and a great community spirit. An excellent brochure covering the Saanich Peninsula and local information is available at the tourist information office on First Street, near the waterfront.

Sidney's waterfront is busy the year 'round, and the shoreline from Sidney northward is well populated with launching ramps, moorings and marinas that provide every conceivable nautical and fishing service. There is also a federal customs and immigration office located in Sidney for the convenience of sea-going visitors.

SIDNEY SPIT MARINE PARK is three miles by water from town. On Sidney Island, it contains 27 campsites and 33 picnic tables.

THE SIDNEY HISTORICAL SOCIETY MUSEUM is found in the old customs building at the foot of Beacon Avenue. It contains an excellent collection of local memorabilia reflecting the early history of North Saanich in particular. Included in the collection is an early edition of Captain Vancouver's journals, antique household and farm items as well as native Indian artifacts. Open to the public from May to September.

15.0 (2.0) JUNCTION: Turn east to approach McDonald Provincial Park via McDonald Park Road.

15.5 (1.5) TOURIST INFORMATION CENTRE. A well run service where you can enquire about accomodations, acquire maps and information about current attractions and activities.

16.2 (0.8) JUNCTION: Turn east to enter McDonald Provincial Park which offers 30 campsites and facilities. Many nearby commercial marinas along the shoreline provide launching, rentals and guide services.

A west turn to Wain Road leads westward to connect with West Saanich road.

16.7 (0.3) BLUE HERON BASIN.

16.9 (0.1) LANDSEND ROAD circles the northern tip of Saanich Peninsula to intersect with West Saanich Road.

17.0 (0.0) SWARTZ BAY FERRY TERMINAL with ferry service to the mainland and Gulf Islands. The 24 mile trip to and from Tsawwassen on the mainland takes an hour and forty minutes to complete.

The mileage figures in brackets are for use by those travelling south from the ferry terminal to Victoria.
To convert to Kilometers, multiply by 1.6.

Two of British Columbia's modern ferries in Active Pass.

The Gulf Islands

THE enchanting chain of islands lying just off the east coast of Vancouver Island in the Strait of Georgia were once a part of the Island but separated from it during centuries of grinding geologic action. The entire archipelago consists of over a hundred islands and extends southward through the International Boundary where the American group are known collectively as the San Juan Islands.

During the past centuries, the abundant fish and wildlife, protected landing beaches, temperate climate, and the proximity of the Gulf Islands to both the mainland and Vancouver Island, made them popular stopping-off points for Nanaimo and Cowichan Indian tribes from Vancouver Island. Salish, Musqueam and Tsawwassens came from the southern mainland, and the fierce northern tribes of Haidas and Bella Bellas made periodic warlike raids on the more peaceable southern tribes. None of these native visitors established permanent settlements in the Islands, and the first recorded settlers were a group of American Negroes who had purchased their freedom in the U.S. and applied to Sir James Douglas for permission to settle on Saltspring Island in 1857.

The topography of the Gulf Islands — a comparatively thin layer of soil covering bare rock — limits the agricultural potential on most of them. Sheep fare well here and several of the islands boast large herds. Truck gardening and orchards are successful on a few islands, but tourism has become a major industry of

143

the Gulf Islands and increasing public and private facilities are geared to serve visitors in hospitable island fashion.

The lure of sheltered, scenic cruising, exciting fishing, and the year-round temperate climate of the Gulf Islands attract thousands of boat owners from the entire West Coast. In fact, the best way to explore some is by boat since many of them are too small for sophisticated road systems, accommodation is apt to be limited, and much of their charm is directly related to the waters that isolate and surround them. The larger islands, as noted here, boast various attractions that will make even a day's excursion a rewarding one.

Most of the parks and campsites mentioned in this chapter are accessible by sea, and the larger islands are tied to each other, the mainland and Vancouver Island by regular ferry service. Passengers travelling on ferries to and from Tsawwassen and Vancouver Island are treated to a close inspection of the fascinating shorelines of the Gulf Islands, especially as the ferries thread their way through Active Pass between Galiano and Mayne Islands. Waterline caves, the multiplicity of meandering inlets and sheltered coves, fleets of sport fishermen — all invite a closer investigation.

SALTSPRING

The largest and most populous of the Gulf Islands, Saltspring is explorable by way of its 100 miles of road, most of it paved, and has three service centres catering to the needs of visitors at Fulford Harbour, Ganges, and Vesuvius Bay. There are many private resorts, some of them spotted among the eleven fresh-water lakes on the island, all of which are well stocked with bass and trout.

Saltspring, which is eighteen miles long and seven miles wide, received its distinctive name after the discovery of fourteen salt springs on the north end of the island. Unlike the low, rolling hills of the other Gulf Islands, Saltspring has steep hills peaking to 2,500 ft. at Mount Bruce which offers a panoramic view of the archipelago. Vancouver Island and the mainland. Two miles south of Ganges on the Fulford Harbour Road, Mount Maxwell Park includes another viewpoint and a small picnic site. On the

144

outskirts of Ganges, Mouat Provincial Park contains fifteen camp-sites and six picnic sites for the use of visitors.

Saltspring, like all the Gulf Islands, is a favoured retirement mecca for Canadians from all parts of the country, and has a permanent population of 4,000 which is more than doubled during the summer months. Agriculture, including the raising of sheep, is still carried on, but it is tourism that now forms the backbone of the island's economy.

Ferry terminals are located at Fulford Harbour, Long Harbour and Vesuvius Bay and can furnish up-to-date schedules for those wishing to do some island-hopping. In addition to water-oriented sports and recreation, Saltspring has golf and riding facilities as well.

GALIANO ISLAND

Considered by many to be the most scenic of the Gulf Islands, Galiano lies between two famous fishing areas. Porlier Pass, on the north, separates it from Valdes Island, and Active Pass, which is also a busy ferry and shipping lane, separates Galiano and Mayne Islands on the south.

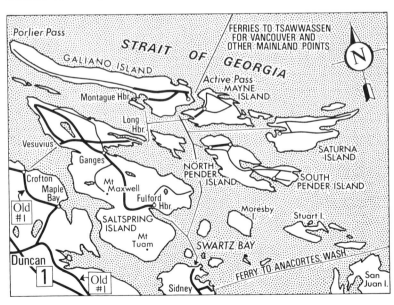

*An early print
showing the
Malispina
Galleries on
Gabriola Island.*

Montague Harbour Marine Park, located four miles west of Sturdies Bay by road, offers 31 campsites, 11 picnic sites, mooring floats, boat launching ramp and excellent swimming. Bellhouse Provincial Park at Sturdies Bay overlooks Active Pass. Private resorts, stores, picnic sites, and a nine hole golf course are available at the southern end of this narrow island.

MAYNE ISLAND

This 8.5 square mile island is a key transfer point in the Gulf Islands ferry system and a popular summer home location for weekend commuters from Vancouver Island and the mainland. There are no public campsites on the island, but accommodation is available at private resorts in and around

146

Village Bay, where shops and marine gas and fuel depots are also centred.

PENDER ISLAND

Although treated as an entity, Pender is actually two islands, North and South Pender, connected by a picturesque, 297 foot bridge. Port Washington, the largest settlement is located near the ferry terminal at the beginning of the cross-island road that terminates at Bedwell Harbour where Canadian Customs maintains a Port of Entry for air and sea craft.

Prior Centennial Park, two miles south of Port Washington, is furnished with 10 campsites, and Beaumont Marine Park on South Pender provides a fine swimming beach close to Bedwell

Harbour Village with its commercial marine and service facilities. There is a nine-hole golf course on North Pender, and the many coves and harbours of rustic South Pender attract many boaters. It was from these coves that rum-runners launched their runs to Seattle during the Prohibition years in the United States.

SATURNA ISLAND

The most south easterly of the Gulf Islands, Saturna has a population of less than two hundred and, as yet, no overnight accommodation for travellers. It does offer a scenic twelve-mile marine drive from the ferry terminal at Lyall Harbour to the East Point lighthouse which is open to the public, and, on the

A glimpse of "peace" in a quiet cove.

148

east slope of Mt. Warburton Pike, an ecological reserve has been established to protect one of the few virgin stands of coastal Douglas firs left in the area. Marine fuel and supplies can be obtained at Lyall Harbour.

Every July 1st, Saturna hosts over a thousand visitors at the annual Saturna Lamb Barbecue which has become a traditional Dominion Day festivity for residents of all the islands.

GABRIOLA ISLAND

Northernmost of the Gulf Islands and lying just east of Nanaimo, Gabriola is a favourite weekend and summer home location for residents of that city. Although the island is only seven miles long, the short ferry trip from Nanaimo gives visitors the opportunity to view the Malaspina Galleries at Descanso Bay. This long, spectacular sandstone formation is an impressive display of the power of the sea on island shorelines.

Cycling on the Gulf Islands is very popular.

149

Sheringham Point lighthouse.

150

Victoria to Sooke and Port Renfrew

SOOKE ROAD (Highway 14) and alternate Metchosin Road are two of the province's oldest roads that, in early days, provided a crucial link for the scattered farms, logging camps, and sawmills of the area with the village and fort at Victoria. To the modern traveller it offers the opportunity to round the southwestern tip of the Island, inspect century-old buildings and communities, enjoy modern or wilderness recreational activities with sweeping views over the Strait of Juan de Fuca opening to the north and west as a reminder of the Pacific beyond.

0.0 JUNCTION of Douglas, Government, Hillside, and Gorge Roads. Proceed onto Gorge Road following Highway 1A for six miles to the start of Highway 14. See map 3.

1.6 TILLICUM ROAD. The entrance to Kinsmen Gorge Park is across the bridge to the left and features swimming and picnicking facilities along the tree-lined promenades edging the Gorge.

The Gorge Waterway runs inland about 3½ miles from Victoria's Inner Harbour. This water route gave first access to the early farm at Craigflower. Portage Inlet at the head of the Waterway is a large, calm, saltwater lagoon. A popular centre of water sports and colorful regattas in earlier days, it still attracts the boaters and fishermen who value its serenity. The shoreline is well suited for a pleasant stroll.

151

2.8 CRAIGFLOWER SCHOOL at Admirals Road was built by the early farmers at Craigflower in 1854. It was the first schoolhouse built in British Columbia and has proved to be the oldest in all western Canada. The school with its original furnishings and class photographs is open to the public. Inquire at the Manor for information.

2.9 CRAIGFLOWER MANOR is a sturdy pioneer home that served as "the big house" for the region's first farm. It is now open to the public and contains an excellent and extensive collection of memorabilia from colonial farm days. It is described more fully in Historic Homes in Victoria on page 00.

4.1 FORT VICTORIA MUSEUM features an accurate reconstruction of one of the two military bastions of Fort Victoria that was built in 1843. The full-scale bastion with its armaments and other exhibits presents an interesting portrayal of life at the early fort centred at what is now Bastion Square in downtown Victoria. This is a private museum but well worth a visit. An admission fee may be charged. See the page 38 picture.

4.4 JUNCTION: Highway 1A briefly joins Highway 1; keep left to continue along 1A.

4.8 6 MILE HOUSE was known as Parson's Bridge Hotel when it opened in 1855 and provided a welcome "rest and refreshment" stop for travellers and horses alike on the then-rugged coach line route along the coast. The name was a tribute to an ambitious early businessman, William Richard Parsons, who operated a grist mill here on the upper reaches of Esquimalt Harbour prior to the construction of the hotel. A sawmill and tannery had also been encouraged to locate their operations in the vicinity.

5.6 JUAN de FUCA CENTRE: One of the finest community Centres on the Island, offering tennis, swimming, and skating, plus lacrosse, soccer and baseball fields. A playground for children and picnic tables add to the pleasant surroundings.

5.8   JUNCTION TO FORT RODD HILL PARK: Now a National Historic Park, Fort Rodd Hill was once an important defense battery guarding the entrance to the Royal Navy Yards at Esquimalt. The installation was first armed in 1895 and the gun batteries and artillery steadily strengthened to form a vital defense system until the accelerated military technology of the post-World War II years rendered shore-based artillery obsolete. Modern museum techniques are used here to interpret the history of the Victoria-Esquimalt coastal defenses from 1878 to 1956.

The Canadian Forces Base at Esquimalt, seen from the protective look-out site of Fort Rodd Hill, today serves as West Coast headquarters for the naval arm of the unified Canadian Forces. Complete with dockyards, moorings, personnel and administration quarters, it is the natural outgrowth of the use made of this sheltered harbour by the British Royal Navy during the decades of exploration.

Fisgard Lighthouse is linked to Fort Rodd Hill by a causeway built in 1950, but is not open to the public since the light, which has been warning ships since 1860, is still operational. Standing 47 feet high, the light beams seventy feet above mean high water level and is visible for ten miles in clear weather. Today the light is operated by automatic equipment. Interpretive displays and guides recount the history of the lighthouse and Fort and the part they played in British Columbia's development.

6.0   COLWOOD JUNCTION marks the start of Highway 14 to Sooke and Port Renfrew. The road was authorized by Governor Douglas in 1852 in order to open up the western lands along the coast and to connect existing farms to the fort at Victoria. "The road to 'Soke' (note original spelling) is progressing favourably", he wrote, "by means of Indian labourers under two white overseers, the labourers being paid at the rate of eight dollars a month." The road must have proved slow and difficult to build however, for much later he commented, "even in its present state, it is passable for horsemen and exceedingly useful for driving cattle."

The Royal Colwood Golf and Country Club nearby was built by James Dunsmuir on the site of "Colwood Farm", the first in the area that had been established by the Puget Sound Agricultural Company. Captain Langford, the bailiff or manager of the farm, named it "Colwood" after the estate he had left in Sussex, England, and played the role of squire in its management and the many social events he hosted there—all enhanced by his five attractive daughters.

6.4   ROYAL ROADS BOTANICAL GARDENS were once part of the fabulous Hatley Park estate of former Premier and Lieutenant-Governor, James Dunsmuir. One of the province's wealthiest men, Dunsmuir invested much of his Island coal, lumbering and shipping profits into the most sumptuous estate west of the Great Lakes. Its 700 acres were set among a majestic fir forest on the slope commanding a panoramic view of the British Navy anchorage at Royal Roads and the entrance to Esquimalt Harbour. The grounds were fashioned into formal Japanese and Italian gardens, promenades, game courts, bridle paths, stables and guest cottages. There were even small lakes stocked with trout for the angling pleasure of the guests. Nearly a hundred Chinese groundskeepers were required to maintain the gardens, and they lived in a "village" of their own in one corner of the estate. An impressive stone and iron wall surrounds the grounds with an ornate gate-keeper's cottage guarding the entrance.

The splendid mansion Dunsmuir built featured a ballroom, conservatory, library, drawing rooms and many guest rooms plus extensive kitchens, dining rooms and a complete laundry. It was completed in 1908 while he was the Lieutenant-Governor of the province and became a major social centre for Victorians.

After the death of Dunsmuir in 1920, his estate proved too expensive to be maintained privately and was eventually sold to the federal government which established the Royal Roads Military College in the mansion and its surrounding grounds. The Botanical Gardens have been preserved as a reminder of the grandeur of Hatley Park and are open daily to the public.

James Dunsmuir's Hatley Castle.

7.4 JUNCTION OF SOOKE AND METCHOSIN ROAD: The Metchosin Road is a fifteen mile alternate route to Sooke that takes the motorist through old farming country interspersed with attractive sea vistas, beaches and parks. Our recommended tour plan would be to travel this route to Sooke or beyond, and then return to Victoria via the Sooke Road.

0.0 METCHOSIN ROAD: Turn left.

1.0 ESQUIMALT LAGOON lies less than one-half mile down Lagoon Road and offers a "water's edge" view of Juan de Fuca Strait. Beachcombing is unusually rewarding here, and a look shoreward across the lagoon gives a magnificent view of Hatley Park and the Royal Roads Military College.

Royal Roads was the name given to the off-shore anchorage used by the British Naval Fleet over a hundred years ago. Modern ships continue to anchor here and can be seen awaiting clearance to enter Esquimalt and Victoria harbours.

2.2 FARHILL ROAD: Turn left to catch a panoramic view of Victoria. Then continue on to Albert Head Lagoon and Wildlife Sanctuary. The beach is a good place for beachcombing and picnicking.

155

4.2 WITTY'S LAGOON PARK: Park and take the trail to the lagoon, or take the approach down Witty's Road a short distance further on. Herons, ducks, geese and swans frequent the lagoon and wildflowers along the trails make this an enjoyable outing. There are lots of picnic sites along the beach. This is but one of the parks created by the Capital Regional District. There are many and they are varied and cater to all outdoor interests.

5.0 JUNCTION WITH HAPPY VALLEY ROAD: Two historical landmarks are located at this intersection; "Saint Mary the Virgin" Anglican Church has been in continuous use at this location since 1873, and the Metchosin Schoolhouse which opened in 1872 has recently been designated as an historic site.

To continue to Sooke, turn right on Happy Valley Road, but the short three mile road straight ahead that ends at the point of land called William Head merits attention.

1.8 DEVONIAN REGIONAL PARK: Longer than it is wide, with trails down through a forested valley to Taylor Beach at Parry Bay. Sherwood Creek flows alongside of the trail and into Sherwood Pond. There are forest, wetland and beach environments to explore, each with an abundance of plant and animal life. Hiking, birdwatching and picnicking can be enjoyed in the park.

2.5 PEARSON COLLEGE OF THE PACIFIC was established on land overlooking Pedder Bay in 1974. Named in honour of the Rt. Hon. Lester B. Pearson, former Prime Minister of Canada. This third link in a chain of six United World Colleges, accommodates 200 students from many countries in the world and enables them to complete their final two years of high school in a stimulating, internationally flavoured environment.

3.0 WILLIAM HEAD: The buildings and grounds now serve as a minimum security prison but are of historical interest because of their earlier use as a federal quarantine station.

Built in 1893, the station was designed to screen the physical health of the thousands of immigrants entering Canada or travelling through to other countries. To quote the Vancouver Daily Province of March 1, 1925, "The vessels have to tarry awhile to give assurance that they do not bring any foreign infection or disease to the people of Canada." Ships were inspected by officials, and if any actual or suspected contagious disease was found, the vessel was forced to dock at the station where passengers were brought ashore for check-ups at the station hospital, the sick treated, and the vessel and its contents fumigated.

It is claimed that upwards of 80,000 Chinese alone passed through the William Head station destined for Canada, the United States and Europe. Many thousands were enroute to France to build roads during World War I.

Modern medicine with more effective control of infectious diseases coupled with the shift to air travel reduced the need for the ship-oriented William Head Quarantine Station and it was closed in 1959. The site on the headland was taken over the same year by the Canadian Penitentiary Service.

5.2 ROCKY POINT ROAD: Turn left off Happy Valley Road.

7.3 MATHESON LAKE: It is one mile to the parking lot and a short hike to this delightful small lake that will yield bass or trout to the fisherman. The beautiful natural surroundings make it an ideal picnic spot and the trail to the far end of the lake makes interesting exploring.

7.4 PEDDER BAY is a narrow inlet that reaches inland for about two miles. This is a popular area for salmon fishing and has a reputation for excellent results when the "runs" are on. It is about one-half mile to the head of the inlet where private boats can be launched or boats and tackle can be rented at the marina.

7.5 JUNCTION: Turn right onto East Sooke Road.

9.0 CHEANUH MARINA is owned and operated by the Beecher Bay Indian Band. Started in 1972 it has complete facilities for boaters and campers. Boats and tackle can be rented or 'ramp' your own boat in. There are campsites, a coffee shop, store and a marine repair shop.

9.5 VIEWPOINT overlooking Becher Bay, the Strait of Juan de Fuca and the open Pacific Ocean beyond. Across the straits the snow-capped Olympic Mountains in Washington State form an impressive backdrop.

10.5 BECHER BAY ROAD: One of the entrances to the East Sooke Park is one mile down this road.

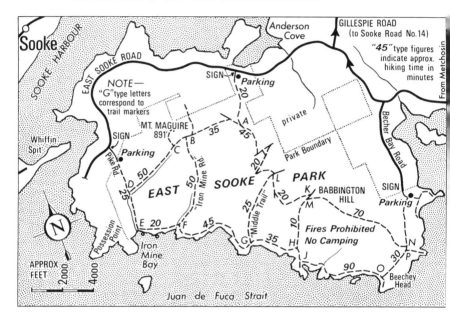

11.7 JUNCTION OF EAST SOOKE AND GILLESPIE ROADS:
A choice of continuing on to Sooke or turning left onto East Sooke Road for an exploration of East Sooke Park.

3.7 EAST SOOKE PARK at Anderson Cove Parking Lot:
Created through the combined efforts of the Provincial Parks Branch and the Capital Regional District, this semi-wilderness area of 3,400 acres gives the visitor a living picture of the typical growth patterns of the competing flora in most coastal forests.

As the accompanying map indicates, trails have been cut and marked as they lead to the Beach Trail. Because of the

158

roughness of the terrain in some areas, the times shown can only be approximate, and it is suggested that hikers travel in pairs and carry some food and drink.

7.6 PIKE ROAD offers another approach to the Park. The parking lot here is closest to the Beach Trail.

15.0 SOOKE ROAD: Turn left to reach Sooke and Port Renfrew, right to Victoria.

The Royal Ensign Hotel is one of the very few "family hostelries" still operating under an old Royal Charter granted to ensure pioneer travellers an hospitable break in their arduous journeys. The hotel was built in 1894 by one Edward Cutler and among the amenities offered was the provision of "hot stones" to warm the feet of the cart and wagon travellers of that era.

SOOKE DISTRICT, as the most southerly end of the Island is known, is a picturesque region with a pleasant mixture of low, green hills and narrow, fertile valleys that are never far from the sandy beaches, quiet bays or rocky headlands of the Pacific.

The thrust of English claims to the area from the east led to the establishment of the first independent settler on the entire Island here in the Sooke District in the person of Captain Walter Colquhoun Grant. In the contract Capt. Grant signed with the Hudson's Bay Company, he agreed to pay one pound sterling per acre and to bring out from England, five men or two couples for every 100 acres he purchased. The farm he founded in 1849 was somewhat smaller than the hundred acres mentioned in his contract, but he had recruited seven men to assist in the clearing and cultivation of the land. Grant, however, was no dedicated farmer, and when several of his men yielded to the lure of the California gold fields, he was not slow to follow. Eventually he returned to England and served brilliantly in Crimean and Indian military campaigns.

Grant left a lasting mark on this area though his own residence in the young colony was relatively brief. During a winter trip to the Sandwich Islands (Hawaii), he was offered some broom seeds by the British Consul there who had cultivated them as a reminder of the "old country". Planted on Grant's farm the following spring, the hardy broom eventually spread throughout the Island, and every spring whole hillsides turn into a golden sea of bloom.

19.3 MILNES LANDING ROAD: A short 3.6 mile trip up the road brings you to the unique Sooke River Potholes Park. Along this section of the river, the action of hard boulders, trapped and swirling on the softer river bedrock, has created the "potholes" that make adventurous swimming holes for hot summer days and that have given the park its appropriate name.

The Sooke River provides cutthroat trout fishing the year round as well as a steelhead season from December to March.

GOLD RUSH TO LEECHTOWN: Approximately ten miles up-stream, the Sooke River is joined by a large tributary, the Leech River. It was at this juncture, on July 26, 1864, that Peter Leech and members of a government exploration party discovered gold. The news brought a rush of gold-seekers and resulted in "instant" Leechtown, a canvas and shanty mining camp, complete with stores, saloons, and hotels to cater to the needs of the more than five hundred men who elbowed for room along the gold-flecked bars of rivers and creeks.

Gold there was, to be sure—by the following spring, more than one hundred thousand dollars in gold had been recovered. Some of the men had made small fortunes; most reaped only blisters and aching backs and gave up. The field proved to be a small one and was soon exhausted. As the miners drifted away, Leechtown disappeared almost as quickly as it had sprung up. Soon only the Gold Commissioner's log house and a few cabins remained, but even these have been overtaken by vandals and the creeping bush. Today, only an historic cairn in the woods is left to mark this mining camp, the scene of Vancouver Island's first, and only, gold rush.

19.8 SOOKE REGION MUSEUM: Exhibits depicting the early days of Sooke help the visitor to visualize the times when early settlers were involved in fishing, sealing, farming and logging in the area, plus the Indian life and culture of the period. Moss Cottage, the oldest existing building in Sooke, is a feature exhibit. The cottage is a 'tidewater house' and the only remaining example of this kind of construction on the Island. Its wide, thick planks were cut in B.C.'s first steam sawmill in 1870. The museum also serves as the tourist information office for the area and is open seven days a week from May through september.

160

Leechtown "accommodation" in 1865.

21.4 SOOKE is the centre of this large farming, fishing and logging area. The harbour is the southernmost in all of Canada. Here fishermen deliver fresh catches of seafood from the Strait and nearby, richly-endowed bays and inlets. Sooke oysters enjoy a reputation for flavour among seafood fanciers.

All Sooke Day, held during July each year, is a tribute to the logging industry and features competitions in high rigging, log birling, axe throwing, and other woods-oriented activities. Loggers from the entire Pacific Northwest converge on Sooke for this renowned event since the world titles earned here are highly valued. Gold Rush days are commemorated as well with "Leechtown" barbecues of beef and salmon.

22.6 WHIFFIN SPIT ROAD is a mile-long drive to the shoreline to a spot ideal for picnics, beachcombing and relaxation. Beyond Sooke, the road travels mainly through wooded areas with frequent spectacular views of the Pacific. Settlement thins out until Jordan River and is sparse again on the road to Port Renfrew. There are a few convenient places to stop with access to the water's edge.

33.1 SHERINGHAM POINT ROAD: The Sheringham Point Lighthouse stands at the end of this one mile road. Built in 1912, it is one of many lights and markers that guide marine traffic through the Straits. Visitors are welcome but only for a limited time each weekday afternoon. See page 150.

33.4 FRENCH BEACH PROVINCIAL PARK has 70 campsites and a number of picnic tables. There is about a mile of pebble beach, ideal for beachcombing and sunbathing.

36.8 POINT NO POINT acquired its unusual name because of the confusion it caused early navigators and hydrographers. From one survey point, it appeared as a prominent headland, while sightings taken from a different direction showed no point at all. In 1895, further surveys designated it "Glacier Point", but local residents preferred the earlier, whimsical name, and, in 1957, their appeal was upheld by the Canadian Geographic Place Names Board who made "Point No Point" the official name.

The wind-sculpted vegetation along the headland adds interest to the trails along the beach and around the point, and there is a small but pleasant lodge to serve visitors.

41.0 JORDAN RIVER lies halfway between Sooke and Port Renfrew at the point where the coast of Vancouver Island begins to curve northward. Both the river and the settlement were named for the Jordan family who arrived from England in 1862 and chose to settle in the remote and isolated coastal forest. For most of its early years, the tiny community served as a logging camp and terminus for a logging railway. In 1911 a power plant was built at Jordan River that by 1913 was producing 26,400 kilowatts of power. Construction of a new plant in 1971, boosted Jordan River's output to 150,000 kilowatts, filling much of the power needs of the southern half of Vancouver Island.

43.5 CHINA BEACH PROVINCIAL PARK: A well-marked trail leads one mile downhill to the beach. Too cold for swimming, it does offer good hiking and beachcombing.

Douglas fir such as these 200 foot giants are now a rarity. A 1910 photo.

50.0 PAVEMENT ENDS, but the fifteen-mile section following is maintained to good gravel road standards.

54.7 LOSS CREEK: A small park is situated at the end of a short, riverside trail.

57.4 SOMBRIO CREEK: Said to be the warmest locality in all of Vancouver Island. Coast Indians used this area as a "spa" for centuries and credited it with powerful, restorative powers.

65.0 PAVEMENT RESUMES.

67.0 PORT RENFREW JUNCTION: Proceed straight ahead for Port Renfrew dock and the village centre. A right turn here leads to the beginning of the B.C. Forest Products logging road and a 32 mile route to Cowichan Lake.

PORT RENFREW is situated at the mouth of the San Juan River. During the 1880s the provincial government of the day attempted to attract settlers to the lush San Juan Valley by offering homestead land within its 10,800 acres and the promise that the road from Victoria to Sooke would be extended on to Port Renfrew. Scores of settlers took up the challenge, and by 1900 there were over 100 settlers in the valley, some of them as far as ten miles up the river. The expense and hard work involved in clearing the land, plus the formidable lack of communications discouraged many and logging has remained the chief industry of the region.

BOTANICAL BEACH: Discovered by a team of botanists in 1894, it has been set aside as a natural, botanical garden that exhibits species of almost every type of West Coast shore life mysteriously assembled in this one area. Inquire locally for directions. Beware of fast-running tide changes that can trap you.

67.4 SAN JUAN RIVER CROSSING.

68.0 SAN JUAN BEACH: A typical, long, open ocean beach.

69.0 CAMPGROUND: Operated by the local Indian Band at the

164

mouth of the river. Inquire here about the excellent sea and river fishing.

69.5 FISHING RESORT: Accommodation and fishing guide services available.

WEST COAST TRAIL: WARNING – due to its hazardous nature, it is strongly advised that competent information be sought before any attempt is made to hike it. Parks Canada has an office nearby where you can get all the advice you need, plus information about water transportation to the starting point. More details can be found on page 182 and 191.

PORT RENFREW TO COWICHAN LAKE AND HIGHWAY 18

Enquire locally to determine if there are any travel restrictions on the road to Cowichan Lake due to logging operations. It is wise to travel with headlights on when on these roads to warn logging trucks and other industrial vehicles of your presence. Be prepared for dusty and sometimes rough road surfaces. Travel slowly. The first 12 miles are paved.

0.0 JUNCTION: Turn right to proceed on this interesting 32-mile drive to the Lake Cowichan road. See the mile 21.3 entry on page 179 of the Duncan to Lake Cowichan and Bamfield chapter.

1.2 DEERING RIVERSIDE PICNIC GROUND

2.8 FAIRY LAKE CAMPGROUND: Not maintained during winter months, but there is good trout fishing at the point where the lake enters the San Juan River.

6.7 JUNCTION: Turn right to Crossover for camping, picnicking and fishing.

6.9 HARRIS CREEK.

7.8 JUNCTION: The right branch leads to prime fishing pools on the upper San Juan River and on to Shawnigan Lake. Turn left for Lizard Lake and Lake Cowichan to the north.

8.9 LIZARD LAKE: Limited campground, good fishing.

11.9 PAVEMENT ENDS.

12.4 HARRIS CREEK CANYON: Proceed straight ahead at junction.

14.4 OLD HARRIS CREEK CAMPSITE: Watch for road signs directing you to swimming and picnic spots.

19.0 JUNCTION: A sharp right turn to exit through the gate leaving B.C. Forest Products land. For the next several miles you will be travelling through areas that have been "logged-off" and replanted.

32.0 JUNCTION AT MESACHIE LAKE: Turn right to reach Lake Cowichan centre.

An early Indian salmon weir on the Cowichan River.

The Old Island Highway

THIS is part of the original highway route of the Island, locally called the Old Island Highway. It served new farms, logging sites, and sawmills as early development spread north from Victoria. Many of the farms and communities along this route are the oldest on the Island. It began as a wagon road from Victoria to Cowichan Bay in 1884.

There is an interesting historical note to the realization of this highway. A notice placed by the government in 1875 read: "The Government of B.C. offer a reward of $100 to any person who will, within three months, measure, distinctly stake out, and blaze the best line for an eighteen foot wagon road, connecting Parson's Bridge, Esquimalt district, with the trunk road at Richardson's farm, on the Cowichan Flats, with gradients not exceeding one foot in ten."

The advertisement went on to require details on bridges required, the extent of swamp covered, character of the land and timber, cribbing and hill cutting required, etc.

With an offer of only $100, at least no one could accuse the government of that day of squandering their funds. A full scale survey today, through 40 miles of virgin forest, could easily run to $250,000. See map 4.

0.0 JUNCTION at Mile 28.5 north of Victoria. The road east will take you to the popular fishing waters of Cowichan Bay and Maple Bay, through the communities of Crofton and

Chemainus, then rejoins the main highway at Ladysmith twenty-four miles north of this junction.

Never very far from the seashore, this pleasant, alternative route has many fascinating points of interest along the way.

0.4 JAMES DOUGAN MEMORIAL: A fitting tribute to early pioneers of the area is this unique family cemetery.

James and Annie Dougan pre-empted 160 acres in this part of Cobble Hill in 1868. By this time the Goldstream Trail had reached Nanaimo, increasing the movement of settlers north from Victoria, and James took the contract to keep the trail passable from Cobble Hill to Goldstream in the south. This and other work, together with his farming, helped the economy of a growing family that was to number eleven sons and two daughters.

2.6 COWICHAN BAY: The Cowichan River, one of the largest on the Island, flows into the head of the bay and here in August and September congregate great numbers of the large Chinook salmon — and fishermen. A month later it is peak season for the Coho salmon. A number of services are available at this centre, boat launches and rentals, restaurants and a small hotel.

4.5 A HISTORIC CAIRN: "To commemorate the landing of the first group of settlers from H.M.S. Hecate at Cowichan Bay at 4 PM on the eighteenth day of August 1862. There were one hundred settlers in the group and his excellency, the Governor, accompanied the expedition."

Typical of these stalwart people, prepared to challenge the unknown, was William John Shearing. Born in 1844 at Kent, England, he went to Hong Kong to work in a law office at age sixteen. Two years later he rejected law as a career and sailed for San Francisco, arriving July, 1862. News of the new British colony developing on Vancouver Island brought him to Victoria in August and on to Cowichan Bay with the other settlers.

Establishing his homestead on the bench above the bay he raised a family and developed a farm out of the wilderness. Like many of the settlers of those early days, he found much needed

168

extra income working for the Government of the day as a foreman on road and bridge work.

ROBERT W. SERVICE, the world renowned poet, came to the Cowichan Valley from England in 1894 at the tender age of seventeen. After a short stint of farm work, he went on to California, returning to the valley in 1901 to work for Mr. George Corfield on the large farm below the Historic Cairn.

First working in the fields, Service eventually filled a vacancy in Mr. Corfield's store and post office; living above the store, he turned a small area into a classroom where he tutored the Corfield's seven sons when there were no customers to wait on. The elevation to these important tasks allowed him to eat with the family in the dining room when previously he had been with the other hired hands in the kitchen.

It was interesting to hear Mr. Fred Corfield, the eldest son, recount from memory how he and Service would take their daily early morning swim in the nearby Koksilah River,

An early view from the present site of the historic cairn with the Corfield store by the roadside.

169

which produced what is purported to be Service's first poem published in Canada. It appeared in the Dec. 5, 1903 issue of the Duncan Enterprise.

> *He stands alone by the water's edge,*
> *With pale and anguished brow,*
> *And shudders as he murmers low:*
> *"It must be done and now."*
>
> *He looks into those icy depths,*
> *With wildly staring eye;*
> *And from his panting breast there breaks,*
> *A deep and bitter sigh.*
>
> *Through all his tense and rigid frame*
> *Great thrills of horror run;*
> *And once again he murmers hoarse:*
> *"It must and shall be done."*
>
> *His mind made up. A long last look!*
> *A plunge! and all is o'er.*
> *He's taken – what was his intent –*
> *His morning bath – no more.*

In 1905 he went to work for the Bank of Commerce in their Victoria branch and was transferred to the Whitehorse, Yukon branch in 1906.

4.9 JUNCTION: Left to the main highway and Duncan. Straight ahead to Maple Bay, Crofton and Chemainus.
Crossing the numerous channels, backwaters and sloughs of the Koksilah and Cowichan rivers, so noticeable on this part of the road, can provide free rein to the imagination as you read the following letter written to Victoria's British Colonist newspaper September 25, 1894.

"I am just returned from Chemainus where I drove some cattle last week. I wish to give warning to all those who may be taking stock in that direction. The trail between this and Cowichan is very bad. There are five sloughs where stock will get

170

mired. The new trail leading across the Cockasilus (Koksilah) River has not a tree blazed, so that the difficulty of finding the track is very great. This river is deep and the banks are steep and miry so that stock have hard work to get out. There are four sloughs almost deep enough to smother any animal that may attempt to cross them. Also, three other rivers where no direction is given of the place you are to cross, or which way the trail runs. I lost more than an hour here seeking to find a way, when an Indian came down the road and showed me".

5.7 TZUHALEM MOUNTAIN: This rocky, high-ridged mass which overlooks Cowichan Bay, took its name from an Indian chief who was born in the 1790s.

Tzouhalem while possessing courage, brains, enterprise and leadership, nevertheless seemed possessed of a demon, for he killed young and old of either sex on the slightest excuse. While others killed for possessions, women and tribal prestige, he left a trail of apparently wanton and senseless murders.

Conducting forays as far away as the area of Tacoma, Washington and Fort Langley up the Fraser River, he was able to escape from his enemies with such ease that he had no difficulty in having followers that believed he had magical powers.

He was finally killed on nearby Kuper Island in 1854 while trying to abduct an Indian woman from her home.

6.1 THE OLD STONE CHURCH: Father Peter Rondeault who came from Victoria by canoe in 1859, built this church in 1864. Kla-ouw-tan was the original Indian name for the low hill on which the church is perched. Here, with the help of the Comiaken Indians and a stonemason from Victoria, the building was "stone by stone" erected. Its walls are almost two feet thick and raised thirty feet high at the gable ends.

Helpers' services were paid in butter which Father Rondeault churned from the milk of his two cows. This led to the church being referred to as the "butter church".

After ten years of use it was abandoned for the villagers wanted it off their property. This led to the building of St. Ann's farther up the road.

171

A very early photograph of the old stone church.

Recently restored and renovated, it is now used by the Cowichan Native Indian Band as a craft centre. The public is welcome to visit and view the crafts and artifacts on display. Watch for the sign directing you up the hill to the parking lot.

7.8 ST. PETER'S CHURCH is one of the many Anglican churches built by early pioneers. Many of these very small but beautiful churches are to be found in "out of the way" settings like this.

John Humphrey was the first European to settle in the Quamichan area. He established a farm and grist mill near here in 1858.

8.0 JUNCTION: The city of Duncan is to the west. Proceed east to Maple Bay, Crofton and Chemainus.

9.0 QUAMICHAN LAKE: This small lake of about 754 acres is good for trolling for rainbow and cutthroat during the spring and fall months. The only access for boats is at the west end at the Art Mann Kin Park on Indian Road. The park has picnic tables and a beach for swimming.

11.1 JUNCTION to Bird's Eye Cove and Genoa Bay. Both of these sites have marinas with all the usual good services.

11.5 MAPLE BAY is just ahead. A turn left will take you on to Crofton and Chemainus.

Maple Bay looks out to Sansum Narrows and the massive bulk of Saltspring Island. The Bay is an excellent place for boating and swimming. A hotel with restaurant and other services overlooks the waters of the bay. There are a few other shops for the convenience of travellers.

13.2 JUNCTION: Continue to Crofton and Chemainus.

15.1 MAPLE MOUNTAIN PARK: It is two and a half miles up to the parking area, from which trails can be hiked to viewpoints overlooking the Gulf Islands and channels to the east. Picnic tables and toilets are on the site. If you are towing a trailer or boat, it is recommended that you leave it down on the main road, for the road, while quite safe and usable, is narrow and steep in places.

16.1 CROFTON: This small community on the slope of land overlooking Osborne Bay is the centre for the surrounding residential and small farm area. A hotel with dining room and other services, motels and a variety of small business establishments serve the community and traveller. The terminal for a ferry service to Vesuvius Bay on Saltspring Island is located at the waterfront.

A huge pile of black slag on the beach gives the clue to the beginnings of Crofton. The Lenora mine on Mt. Sicker, about four miles to the west, was developed by a Henry Croft. He decided to build a smelter here at tidewater in 1902 and feed it with ore transported from the mine over a narrow gauge railroad. Other mines in the region also shipped their ore to his smelter.

This activity was enough to sprout a boom town almost overnight. However, around 1907 the smelter was in difficulties due to the drop in copper prices and the fact that the ore was proving too expensive to treat. These various factors combined to close it in 1908 and the town folded with it. Not long after, the smelter was completely destroyed by fire. The mine continued to produce however, and realized over a million dollars in copper, zinc and gold.

In the decades that followed, many persons looking for a pleasant country atmosphere settled in the scenic Crofton area.

16.5 JUNCTION: Turn west to continue on to Chemainus.

17.2 VIEWPOINT: A short distance down the road for an excellent look at the pulp mill and Osborne Bay.

17.4 CROFTON PULP MILL: Established in 1957, this B.C. Forest Products Company mill produces slightly less than 1,000 tons of kraft pulp per day; 150 tons are used to make newsprint. Sixty miles of newsprint are turned out every hour by two modern paper machines.

Some 1,000 employees work at the mill, docks and lumber assembly wharf, producing and shipping annually over 20,000 tons of pulp and newsprint and 250 million board feet of lumber.

18.9 JUNCTION: Continue north to Chemainus.

19.2 CHEMAINUS RIVER.

19.3 ALL SAINTS WESTHOLME: This picturesque little Anglican church held its first service on May 30, 1880.

22.5 CHEMAINUS: For over one hundred years a sawmill has stood on the sheltered shore of this bay, and gathered around it a community which draws its lifeblood from the logs which are moved methodically through the mill processes.

A giant in today's forest industry, this MacMillan Bloedel Company operation would be a marvel to the men who built the first mill. They got their power from a water wheel and a labour force of two. Now the average daily production is far more than was produced in a year of those earlier days.

Sailing ships loading lumber at Chemainus in the early 1900s.

Daily tours are conducted and should be high on the list of "things to do."

When the recession of the 80's curtailed lumber production, the economics of 'lumber towns' was indeed grim and Chemainus was no exception. With employment at a near standstill, the effect on the town was drastic. But the spirit and determination to do something about it resulted in Chemainus becoming known as "The Little Town That Did", receiving the prestigious "First Place Award" in the 1983 New York based downtown revitalization competition.

Throughout this unique town twelve "larger-than-life" murals that have been painted on the sides of buildings, recount the town's proud past. Scenes of old donkey engines, steam locomotives and other pioneer activities, etc., back up the town's claim to having Canada's largest permanent outdoor art gallery.

It is a further six miles to where this road rejoins the main Island highway; a pleasant drive through small farm and residential sections, terminating at Mile 28.5 just south of Ladysmith.

A pause for a family portrait during a 1893 visit to a logging area.

Duncan to Lake Cowichan and Bamfield

Within its first 25 miles, Highway 18 serves the logging and lumbering communities of Lake Cowichan, Youbou, Mesachie Lake and Honeymoom Bay.

Beyond is a vast hinterland of rugged mountains and narrow valleys containing many rivers and lakes and always the evidence of forestry operations.

The first 25 miles is paved public road, beyond that are the private logging roads that vary from well graded gravel to rough stony surfaces. The latter are open for public use subject to conditions laid down by the logging companies. It is wise to acquire maps and local information before proceeding on them.

0.0 HIGHWAY 18 proceeds west from a junction on the main Island Highway three miles north of Duncan. See maps 4 and 5.

1.0 MT. PREVOST looms above on the right. The huge pylon on its 2,600 foot peak is a war memorial to Cowichan Valley residents who gave their lives in the two world wars.

For the next ten miles the road passes through an interesting forest of young evergreens, interspersed with a wide variety of deciduous growth. Particularly noticeable is the extensive grove of alder at about Mile 11.

7.2 PICNIC AND REST AREA.

177

9.5 **C.V.D.F.:** One-half mile to a parking lot and the starting point of trails through the woods to a number of descriptive signs that explain the nature of forest ecology. The whole family will find this instructive and enjoyable.

11.8 SKUTZ FALLS on the Cowichan River is a short distance down this road. This picturesque section of the river is good for fishing and rambling.

16.1 JUNCTION: Youbou is ten miles along the north side of the lake. Site of a large sawmill and veneer plant.

16.4 TOURIST INFORMATION CENTRE: Here you can acquire information on the location of boat access to the lake and other local activities. Enquire about public tours of the nearby Satellite Earth Station operated by Teleglobe Canada.

16.8 LAKE COWICHAN: Population 2,364. 1912 was the year that the first townsite was planned and building lots sold. This was also the year that the E. and N. railway branch line arrived. Prior to this, settlers were coming into the area in the 1880s. The then Premier, William Smythe, when asked about the possibility of building a road from Duncan to the Lake said, "If you can get ten or a dozen settlers up there the road will be built." It was constructed in 1885 under a contract of $100 per mile.

The community has provided two excellent picnic sites in the centre of town. Additionally there are a number of stores and other services to satisfy the visitor's needs.

Be sure to visit the excellent museum housed in the abandoned railway station.

21.0 MESACHIE LAKE is best known as the former site of the Hillcrest Lumber Company. Founded by Carlton Stone in 1917, the Company first located near Duncan. Here it established an enviable reputation as a forerunner in the development of lumber exports to the United Kingdom in the 1930s. Particularly successful were their efforts to introduce hemlock as a satisfactory soft wood to this market in competition with supplies from Scandinavian countries.

Depleted timber stocks in the area brought about a move in 1943 to Mesachie Lake, where for the next 25 years the operation logged and processed well over a billion board feet from the more than 20,000 acres available to them.

Timber reserves ultimately proved insufficient to support the three large mills in the area, so Hillcrest, reluctantly was faced with an ultimate end to their enterprise. Operations ceased in 1968—the end of nearly half a century of a highly successful family business.

All that remains is a large storage shed, the office building and acres of open land that once housed one of the most respected sawmill operations in British Columbia. Many of the items of equipment were donated to the Forest Museum near Duncan, including steam locomotives that hauled the cars of logs from bush to mill.

The village, created by the Stone family for their employees, is still to be seen and a visit to the unique rustic inter-denominational church will be rewarding.

FORESTRY RESEARCH has been conducted at the nearby provincial research station since 1929. Genetic improvement plus increased growth and yield of second-growth Douglas fir is the scientific pursuit on this large site overlooking Cowichan Lake. Watch for the sign directing you to this intriguing place where the public is welcome to learn of the various experiments being conducted.

21.3 JUNCTION to Port Renfrew, see page 166. Acquire a copy of the Visitors Guide Map from the B.C. Forest Products Office here.

22.0 ASHBURNHAM BEACH: It is a short distance down to the lake and an excellent picnic site provided by B.C. Forest Products Co.

LOG-SORT GROUNDS: Timber from the nearby logging operations are brought to this huge area for sorting and scaling. Watch out for fast-moving logging trucks and drive with your headlights on.

23.2 HONEYMOON BAY: Named by a Mr. March who brought his new bride to open up a homestead here on the lakeshore.

24.6 JUNCTION: Bear right to reach the provincial government's Gordon Bay Campground on the shore of the lake, has 130 campsites, a boat launching ramp and an RV sani-station.

COWICHAN LAKE is one of the largest on the Island. With some 64 miles of shoreline it and its feeder streams drain approximately 235 square miles of country. It is about 25 miles long and one mile wide. Fishing is good for cutthroat, rainbow and Dolly Varden trout.

Bear left at this junction to continue to Nitinat and Bamfield.

25.0 WILDFLOWER PRESERVE: Watch carefully for a small sign that directs you in to the left. Western Forest Industries Company have set aside this area and provided trails through the woods for the public to enjoy the more than 25 species of wildflowers that can be seen at different seasons.

25.6 PAVEMENT ENDS: From this point mileages can be calculated as follows; Caycuse 9.0 miles, Nitinat Lake 35.0 and Bamfield 67.0. Be sure that you have good tires if you are going to continue on to Bamfield. The trip is worthwhile but some sections can have loose sharp rock in which case – travel slowly.

28.2 LOG BRIDGE: At the bottom of a hill where the road makes a sharp horseshoe bend, watch for an old logging bridge that nature is gradually taking over.

30.3 CAYCUSE CAMPGROUND: Provided by B.C. Forest Products Company, this excellent park contains about 25 campsites, picnic tables, a nature trail, swimming and boat launching ramp.

35.1 CAYCUSE: Headquarters for B.C. Forest Products Cowichan logging division where there is a coffee shop, store, pay phone, gas pump and boat ramp available to the public. If you are proceeding on to Bamfield or Port Alberni, this is the last opportunity to obtain some of these services.

35.9 JUNCTION: Turn right for Nitinat and Bamfield.

The first record of white explorers to the Cowichan Lake area was a party under a Mr. Pemberton that landed at Cowichan Bay in 1857 from Victoria and travelled up river to the lake and then on to Nitinat. Pemberton enthused on the quality of the timber, and the abundance of elk, deer, grouse and fish.

40.3 JUNCTION: Continue straight ahead for Nitinat Lake and Bamfield. Turn right to reach the nearby B.C. Forest Products Heather campground. Here are facilities for swimming and overnight camping. There is a boat ramp and a sani-station for camper-trucks.

44.4 LOOKOUT: To the right of the road is a view into a wooded valley and hills beyond. Notice the "cap" of timber left on one of the hills; this is to provide for natural seeding of surrounding areas.

45.2 GATE: Leaving B.C. Forest Products operations and entering MacMillan Bloedel Franklin River Division.

47.6 TIMBER HARVESTING: In this general area, examples of the methods used in controlled cutting and re-planting can be seen.

52.0 JUNCTION: Take the left fork to reach Nitinat Lake and MacMillan Bloedel's public campground with 12 campsites, a picnic site and boat launching ramp. There is also a picnic site on the Nitinat river on the way to the lake. Continue right for Bamfield or Port Alberni.

52.4 NITINAT RIVER: Fair trout fishing year-round and steelhead runs in the fall and winter. Look for the spectacular falls on the river at about this point.

56.7 Continue straight ahead eight miles to Franklin Camp. From Franklin it is 26 miles to Port Alberni and 30 miles to Bamfield.

FRANCIS AND DARLINGTON LAKES offer good fishing for trout.

65.0 FRANKLIN CAMP: Headquarters of MacMillan & Bloedel's Franklin/Sarita logging operations. Drive cautiously, with headlights on and watch out for fast-moving logging trucks.

72.0 SARITA RIVER flows into and out of Sarita Lake. Good trout fishing.

74.0 SARITA LAKE: Boat launching for cartop boats. Good fishing for Cutthroat, Dolly Varden and Kokanee.

83.0 POETT NOOK MARINA is 2½ miles from this junction. You will find a full range of facilities for camping and fishing at this well-run and tidy marina.

THE WEST COAST TRAIL, beginning at Pachena Bay, this old lifesaving access route follows the Island's wild storm-swept coastline for 45 miles. The Dominion Government in 1890 installed a telegraph line along the trail to lighthouses at Carmanah Point and Cape Beale, so that impending or actual ship-wrecks could be reported to Victoria. Survivors could follow the trail to small cabins equipped with telephones and emergency supplies. With the advent of modern rescue methods and com-munications, the trail is no longer maintained for this purpose. Today it is suitable for hardy wilderness hikers who can ford cold creeks, make good time through dense rainforests, and properly judge the tides where travel on the beaches is necessary. For less qualified hikers, the first six miles leading to Pachena Point Lighthouse are in good condition. The lighthouse was built in 1907. It stands 200 feet above the sea and is visible for 20 miles, one of the most powerful lights on the coast.

PARKS CANADA have an information and registration centre at the bay for the benefit of hikers wishing to use the trail.

West Coast Trail hikers must frequently endure wet conditions.

89.5 PACHENA BAY ROAD. There is a large number of campsites available and the hard-packed sandy beach is excellent for swimming and sunbathing.

90.0 FOOTBRIDGE: This suspension bridge over the Pachena River is typical of many that existed on the west coast before roads were put through.

91.0 BAMFIELD: Named after William Eddy Banfield who was a carpenter on H.M.S. "Constance". He took his discharge in 1849 and became one of the first European settlers in the area. For some reason, the differences in spelling were never corrected.

For these many years Bamfield has been a centre for one of the fishing fleets of the west coast of the Island. Additionally it is one of the bases of the lifeboat service that has been available to mariners in distress out in the open waters of the Pacific Ocean.

183

Bamfield's major contribution to history however, began with the decision to establish it as the western terminus of a trans-Pacific communication cable. September 19, 1902 saw the beginning of this project, when the cable ship "Colonia" started laying the 4,000 mile cable from Bamfield to Fanning Island, a tiny coral atoll in mid-Pacific near the equator. There it was connected to a link with Australia and put into service November 1, 1902.

A connecting cable was laid to Port Alberni in 1959, at which time the Bamfield station was closed.

A new and modern cable was laid from Port Alberni to Hawaii in 1963. Unlike the original which transmitted one message at a time, at a speed of eight words per minute by key, this new cable contains eighty voice channels.

The cable station building has been taken over by a complex of three British Columbia universities and two Alberta Universities and turned into a marine sciences centre. Here staff and students are conducting marine biology research under ideal conditions provided by the unique ocean conditions prevailing in the area.

On this remote and rugged west coast there is limited accommodation or other services available but there are great shorelines for beachcombing and trails to explore before you return to civilization.

The Bamfield Cable Station in the early 1900s.

Parksville to Port Alberni and the West Coast

DURING the 1880s, pioneers in the already-settled communities of Coombs, Errington, Hilliers and Port Alberni were pressing for a route from the east coast of the Island to Port Alberni on the west. This road was built in 1886 and ended the isolation of settlers who, until then, had to travel overland on horseback, or rely on infrequent, and often dangerous, boat service down the west coast to reach Nanaimo or Victoria.

Today, the road is highlighted by deep, virgin stands of Douglas fir at Cathedral Grove and, once past Port Alberni, provides the traveller with a wide-lens panorama of logging activity conducted on near-perpendicular hillsides. Extensive glacial movement, forest fires and logging have left spectacular, visible scars on the austere, uninhabitable land traversed before the road winds down to the coastal lowlands. Here the visitor will be greeted by the wild surf of the open Pacific at sandy Long Beach, part of the new Pacific Rim National Park, and the two, attractive fishing ports of Tofino and Ucluelet.

0.0 PARKSVILLE: Turn west onto Highway 4 at the main junction. See map 5.

0.1 ROD AND GUN HOTEL: Behind the modern face lies one of the older buildings in the district. It was built in 1895 and has kept the same name through the years.

1.5 THE HALFWAY HOUSE provided much welcomed meals

185

Hiker and mountaineer alike should be aware that on the finest day, Mt. Arrowsmith can suddenly become shrouded in clouds.

and lodgings for travellers between Nanaimo and Alberni. In the late 1890s, when fire claimed the original structure, a replacement was built which survived into the 1960s. Typical of its architecture is the building noted below, at Coombs.

3.0 ENGLISHMAN RIVER FALLS PARK is one of the most popular provincial parks on the Island. It is five miles south of Highway 4 and centres on a half-mile of the river distinguished by crystal clear pools, two waterfalls, and a deep canyon gorge. The lower pool is a natural "swimmin' hole" for those who like a brisk plunge. The park's facilities include 100 campsites and 37 picnic sites.

4.7 MOUNT ARROWSMITH standing prominently to the west, is the highest mountain in the southern portion of the Island. Its summit ramparts, always laced with snow, rise to 5,962 feet, high above the Alberni basin. A regional park and ski area has been developed on its north flank; access road is at mile 22.0.

5.3 COOMBS: An old pioneer community and stopping point on the stage route to Alberni. The log house and barn on the south side were built at the turn of the century.

8.4 JUNCTION: Turn north for Helliers (0.4 miles) and Qualicum Beach (5.0 miles). This is a "cut-off" road between the two major highways. An early English settler, Thomas Hellier, gave this farming district its name.

10.3 WHISKEY CREEK and nearby Tranfield Swamp were the favoured range of a band of elk at the turn of the century. They wintered in these lowlands, away from the more heavily-snowed mountains, finding grazing on the meadow grasses. The herd was seriously decimated by early settlers, and only a few remain in inaccessible areas on Vancouver Island.

11.2 LITTLE QUALICUM FALLS PARK has an excellent campground at 0.2 miles and the main parking lot is at 0.8 miles. 100 individual campsites, and scores of tables for picnickers, testify to the popularity of this park. There are several places where one can swim, and the river above and below the immediate park area provides fair to good trout fishing.

13.7 CAMERON LAKE PICNIC SITE is a very scenic location, fronting on a gravel beach near the east end of the lake. For the next three miles the highway follows the shore of this deep mountain lake. There is fishing for small trout, averaging one pound.

15.0 BEAUFORT PICNIC SITE is situated out on the nearby point.

17.2 MACMILLAN PARK: This deep, stately forest, known as "Cathedral Grove", is one of the few surviving primeval, uncut stands of timber that may be seen by the travelling public. Once most of this Island was covered with such trees and their accompanying range of plant and wildlife species.

The finest portion of the forest is a majestic grove of Douglas Fir, Western Hemlock, Grand Fir, and Western Red Cedar. A half-hour loop walk threads through from the parking area and leads to one giant tree over nine feet thick and 250 feet high. Sword Fern and Maidenhair Fern provide a luxuriant ground cover, and occasionally a deer may be seen.

You cannot fully appreciate this timeless setting except by leaving your car and taking a walk through nature's cathedral. There is parking area at 17.7 miles.

21.8 PASS: Both the highway and railway reach an elevation of 1,272 feet here, crossing the southern highlands of the Beaufort Range.

22.0 MOUNT ARROWSMITH PARK: Some 1,500 acres of excellent alpine terrain is the site of an excellent ski hill, with T-bars and rope tows and a fine mix of slopes for all calibre skiers. A day lodge, cafeteria and rental shop will cater to your needs.

During the summer months hiking is particularly appealing, with breathtaking views north and eastward along the Island's east coast and across the Strait of Georgia to the mainland.

188

A short twelve mile drive will bring you to a viewpoint where you can park and enjoy the alpine scenery or do some hiking.

23.0 OLD TRAIL TO COWICHAN LAKE: An important travel route for a few years in the 1890s was this trail from the Port Alberni region south to Cowichan Lake. There was a relatively large settlement in the Cowichan Valley, so it was only natural that there would be a clamour for a trail between the two points. This was built in 1892-1893 and was 38 miles long.

A traveller of those days reports: "For the whole of the way we found what might be best called an unfinished wagon road. There are stretches for miles where a buggy might be driven with ease, then again where it would be utterly impossible."

Today you may sample part of the trail by making an easy 1½ hour loop walk, beginning at a point around the end of a locked gate at the bottom of an old section of highway in this vicinity. Information on this and other hiking trails are outlined in a guide available at the tourist information centre.

26.3 JUNCTION: Highway No. 4 continues on the right fork to Ucluelet, Long Beach and Tofino. The left fork leads to the Port Alberni city centre. The **TOURIST INFORMATION CENTRE** at this junction is a worthwhile stop to acquire information about the city and surrounding countryside. This well-run centre can supply you with maps and acquaint you with all the fine travel and recreation opportunities offered in the region.

If you plan to go on to Long Beach or Bamfield you should get advice on accomodations and road conditions, etc.

28.9 PORT ALBERNI, population 32,558: Turn left for city centre, or turn right to rejoin Highway 4 to the west coast. The city region was first settled in 1860, when nine men landed ashore to construct the first sawmill in British Columbia for cutting export timber. In November of 1864, the mill manager notified the Colonial Secretary that "the decision to place a sawmill at the head of Alberni Inlet has proven disastrous, for there is no wood in the district to supply the wants of a large mill." 104 years later, in 1969, 228 deep-sea vessels left the harbour laden with 253 million f.b.m. (feet board measure), including 335,679 tons of paper, 60,651 tons of pulp, 43,976 tons of plywood, 2,147 tons of shingles, and 908 tons of miscellaneous lumber.

The name Alberni was first applied to the settlement at the head of the long inlet which almost severs central Vancouver Island, by Captain Richards of H.M.S. "Hecate" in 1861, in acknowledgment of a Spanish party which explored the area seventy years before. Large scale development and settlement did not evolve until after creation of what is now MacMillan and Bloedel's Alberni Pacific Division Sawmill in 1904, and again not until 1947 when one of Canada's most productive pulp and paper mills was established. Products today are milled and finished out of the raw timber, then dispatched by rail and sea through Port Alberni's sophisticated port facilities. Mill tours are generally available Monday through Friday.

Roger Creek Park is in the centre of town, and in summer it offers quiet shade, a "swimmin' hole" right in the creek, a wading pool, picnic tables, and restrooms.

CHINA CREEK PARK is nine miles southwest of the city on tidewater. It is a tenting area provided by MacMillan and Bloedel Limited, featuring a cook-out shelter, boat ramp, and fuel. This provides ready access to Alberni Inlet and Barkley Sound—both areas have Tyee and Coho salmon fishing in season.

Although Port Alberni is a deep-sea port, it is some forty miles inland from the Pacific Ocean, at the head of the Inlet. The surroundings are mountainous, with several large valleys whose slopes retain virgin stands of timber. In cleared areas various types of agriculture are applied, with the emphasis on dairy farming.

ONE—DAY FERRY EXCURSIONS down the Alberni Inlet are available aboard the M.V. "Lady Rose," going to either Bamfield or Ucluelet on certain days from the Argyle Street Dock. The trip down this fjord and through the Barkley Sound region offers magnificent ocean scenery.

THE WEST COAST TRAIL, beginning some three miles south of Bamfield at Pachena Bay, is an old lifesaving access route which follows the Island's wild storm-swept coastline for

45 miles. The Dominion Government in 1890 installed a telegraph line along the trail to lighthouses at Carmanah Point and Cape Beale, so that impending or actual shipwrecks could be reported to Victoria. Survivors could follow the trail to small cabins equipped with telephones and emergency supplies. With the advent of modern rescue methods and communications, the trail is no longer maintained for this purpose. Today it is suitable for hardy wilderness hikers who can ford cold creeks, make good time through dense rainforest, and properly judge the tides where travel on the beaches is necessary. For less qualified hikers, the first six miles leading to Pachena Point Lighthouse are in good condition.

29.2 STAMP FALLS PARK JUNCTION is reached by continuing on Highway 4 from the junction at mile 26.3. The park is located about eight miles along the Beaver Creek road. This provincial campground has 20 campsites, and an additional sixteen picnic tables. There is a lovely waterfall, named after Captain Edward Stamp who had supervised the establishment of the earliest mill at Alberni. During the summer and fall visitors can watch salmon ascending fish ladders. There are walks to several scenic spots and fishermen can cast for steelhead and cutthroat trout.

SPROAT LAKE and the mountains of the Beaufort Range.

191

29.4 SOMASS RIVER has a boat launching ramp at River Road and Beaver Creek Road. The former includes a park with picknicking, swimming, and a playground. Further up Falls Road is Paper Mill Dam Park, the site of British Columbia's first paper mill, offering similar attractions. Both facilities are provided by the municipality.

34.1 SPROAT FALLS BRIDGE crosses the Somass River, which is Sproat Lake's outlet to Alberni Inlet. In days long past, the Indians camped here while catching and smoking migrating salmon. You can drive off on a side road and from the open setting of mossy rocks picnic or try the fishing. There is a fish ladder at the main falls.

35.4 GREAT CENTRAL LAKE JUNCTION: The lake is reached by turning right and driving five miles. It is 22 miles long, averaging a mile and a half in width, and its recreational attributes include boating, water skiing, swimming, and year-round fishing for cutthroat and Kamloops trout (although March through October is best for this). Camping and picnicking sites, rental boats, cabins and other facilities are available here.

Capable hikers can venture into the southern wilderness of Strathcona Park by taking a boat to the west end of Great Central Lake, and from there proceeding along Drinkwater Creek via a poor road and undeveloped trail for ten miles to the base of Della Falls. This is an alternate route to that mentioned on page 210, where this remarkable cascade is described.

35.5 SPROAT LAKE PROVINCIAL PARK has 40 campsites and 146 picnic tables, and offers boating, water skiing, swimming (a change house is provided), and good fishing for cutthroat and rainbow trout from April to November. There is a boat launching ramp onto the lake, which is seventeen miles long and a mile wide.

40.0 TREE FARM: This large logged area has fed the mills at Port Alberni for many years. The uniform stands of re-growth are planted seedlings, raised in forestry nurseries where selective breeding produces hardier, faster-growing trees. Much

Water bombers can be seen at their base on Sproat Lake. These huge aircraft are 120 feet long, have a wing span of 200 feet and weigh 51 tons. They are designed to carry 30 tons of chemically treated water used to "bomb" forest fires.

of this section was replanted in 1955. On either side of the lake can be seen the steep switchback roads characteristic of logging operations. Such roads are the only access to considerable areas of Vancouver Island.

In this region you can also see the various kinds of shrubs and flowers that take root in the exposed land; common species are huckleberry, dogwood, alder, ferns, and the pretty blue lupine. Old stumps indicate the grandeur of the original timber removed from this area, and occasional survivors of the early forest can still be seen near the road.

54.0 GLACIAL ACTION is very evident here. A massive and heavy valley glacier, with rocks imbedded in its base, scoured the area, leaving large polished faces and lateral "stria" or scratches on the exposed bedrock. The last glacier melted away from this area perhaps 10,000 years ago (very recently by a geologist's time scale) when, in human history, man was decorating caves in Europe and learning to grow his food. Almost all of Vancouver Island was affected in similar fashion by glacial

Glacial era boulders in the Kennedy River.

action—the result can be seen in the dramatically sharpened peaks, the steep side-cut valleys, the lack of topsoil, the large "erratics" or boulders deposited along valley floors, and "drowned" valleys captured by the sea after the ice retreated to form fjords. In the highest mountain areas of the central Island, some small, active glaciers still remain.

55.8 TAYLOR RIVER Valley is strewn with erratics, and on the slopes you can see what was left by a devastating forest fire. Many of the dead trees have been removed to make room for re-growth, leaving only blackened stumps. In the early spring cutthroat trout can be taken from this river.

194

For the next five miles, the road crosses the divide between east and west-flowing rivers, through Sutton Pass.

61.0 KENNEDY RIVER races alongside the road for eighteen miles, swelling with waters from freshets and creeks until it empties into the lake. Cutthroat trout often can be caught in quiet pools in the river.

79.0 KENNEDY LAKE is the Island's largest. Its horseshoe-shape covers 24 square miles. Good trout fishing is usually found at the mouth of creeks flowing into the lake.

83.0 BOAT LAUNCHING from a small, pebbled beach.

84.0 LAKESHORE BEACH that is popular for swimming and picnics is located at the end of a short road.

89.0 JUNCTION: Left to Ucluelet, right to Tofino. Mileages to Tofino start on page 200. Fourteen miles between this junction and Tofino is National Park territory and no commercial facilities are available for supplies.

THE PARK INFORMATION CENTRE is located 1.5 miles to the right of this junction. The staff can offer advice, maps and brochures on the park and its services. There is also a fine display of interpretive material for your information.

UCLUELET INLET: At its head is a dumping and booming ground for logs harvested from the nearby hills. When weather and tides are right, the booms are towed up Alberni Inlet to the timber-hungry mills at Port Alberni. The Inlet also creates narrow Ucluth peninsula.

5.0 UCLUELET is a very old fishing port and settlement situated on a valuable shelter from the periodic rampages of the Pacific yet close to the great banks and channels where migrating salmon feed. The area was settled long ago in prehistoric times. Its name derives from "yu-clutl-ahts", meaning "the people with a good landing place for canoes". Now it is a large fleet of trollers, rather than canoes, that seek the Inlet's quiet waters. Their numbers swell considerably at the height of the fishing season. Ucluelet is one of B.C.'s top ports in volume of landed salmon, and the village keeps busy servicing this fleet and handling the large catch. Here are fish camps, gas docks, cold storage plants, wharves, ways and repair depots supporting the industry.

Port Albion on "the other side" was established in the 1880s by the first white settlers in the area just along from the Indian village at the Inlet's entrance. When more settlers arrived, they found the cheapest land lay on the west side and founded the present townsite there.

Fishing, and later, logging, provided the community's economic base, but many newcomers also tried farming or panning for gold at Wreck Bay. But the gold was too scattered and fine, and the land too acidic and rain-leached for farming so fishing has proved to be the reliable, stable industry that supports most of the village.

Like Tofino, Ucluelet relied on coastal steamers for regular communication and supplies, and today the village still gets

Ucluelet, with Long Beach on the open Pacific in the distance.

196

steamer service from the "Lady Rose", a passenger and freight ship headquartered at Port Alberni.

The village was incorporated in 1952, and in 1959, the long-awaited road to Port Alberni was completed after sixty years of promises and intermittent construction. Now tourism, a formidable by-product of the improved road and the new national park, has become a major industry and stimulation to the village's growth.

AMPHITRITE POINT AND LIGHTHOUSE (48 deg. 55'17" North latitude; 125 deg. 32'23" West longitude) is a short drive past the village at the tip of the peninsula overlooking the rock-strewn "ship's graveyard" entrance to Barkley Sound. A

The "Vanlene" on the rocks at the entrance to Barkley Sound.

sample of the scores of tragic wrecks in this area would include: H.M.C. Minesweeper, "Thiepval" which sank in the Sound in 1932; the "Pass of Melfort" which sank off Amphitrite Point in 1905; the "Florencia" which sank, in 1861, off Florencia Island in what is known locally as Wreck Bay, and just recently, the "Vanlene" which sank off Austin Island in 1972. These were great, ocean-going ships, not the smaller, local craft that also brave these treacherous waters—all mute testimony to the savage fury of a Pacific storm. The frequency of wrecks led to the establishment of lifeboat stations at Tofino, Ucluelet and Bamfield and the clearing of the 45 mile "Lifesaving Trail" along the empty coastline to the south.

Amphitrite Light has been flashing nightly every fifteen seconds since 1905, guiding mariners up to 13 miles at sea; the three-second blast/27 second silent, foghorn has been warning ships since 1927.

The Tofino Traffic Centre, operated by Transport Canada, assists ships in making a safe landfall to the west coast and guides them safely into the Strait of Juan de Fuca, where the Vancouver Traffic Control provides assistance for ships heading through both Canadian and United States waters to their final destinations. Enquire about tours of this fascinating operation.

PACIFIC RIM NATIONAL PARK presents a wide variety of dramatic landscapes—long, sandy beaches, quiet estuaries, surf-swept headlands, thick rain-forests, rocky islands, and the never-ending sweep of the Pacific Ocean. The park is shared by pods of whales travelling offshore, flocks of geese migrating along the flyway, and all manner of life in the regions between— in the damp spruce forests, over the wide beaches and estuaries, on the rookeries offshore, and in the gently swaying kelp forests beneath the sea. It is truly an outstanding natural environment, now securely preserved as parkland, here on the rim of the Pacific.

The Park covers approximately 150 square miles of land, divided into three basic and distinct areas, all in various stages of development.

THE BROKEN ISLANDS in the mouth of Barkley Sound form the second area of the park, and are the least visited. These 98 scattered islands, rocks, and reefs support rich sealife, gale-stunted trees, private rookeries of thousands of birds and herds of sea lions.

THE WEST COAST TRAIL, stretching 45 miles south from Bamfield to Port San Juan is the historic feature of this section of the Park. Originally built to aid shipwrecked mariners, the trail now introduces hardy hikers to the rugged, lonely stretches of rocky shore and deep forest that is typical of the Island's west coast. See page 191.

Park boundaries, and consequently, certain park features,

Sea lions off Long Beach.

are still under negotiation, but most current activity and development has been in the popular Long Beach area.

LONG BEACH is the major section of the park and is made up of about 56 square miles of forest, estuary, and beach—teeming with life. Between the forest and the sea, Long Beach with its broad expanse of hard-packed sand and steady drumroll of breakers attracts thousands of visitors.

There is so much to see and do in the Long Beach section of the Park, that it would be impossible to adequately inform you in this brief space. Two stops are important, the Information Centre at mile 1.5 from the junction and the Museum and Interpretive Centre at Wickaninnish Bay 4.5 miles from the junction. In both places you will be provided with complete details about this National Park and all it has to offer.

Park naturalists have set up an interpretive program designed to acquaint visitors with the Park's various components: land, water, plants, and animals—all interacting in a life-cycle that forms the Park's total environment. They invite participation in these programs, some of which involve short one or two mile hikes.

If you need accomodation or plan to camp, there are in addition to the Park campsites, motels at Ucluelet and Tofino plus tent, R.V. and cottage facilities at Mackenzie Beach and a large, full-facility R.V. Park and campground at Cox Bay.

Both Ucluelet and Tofino have many current attractions and historical points of interest to intrigue the visitor. Consider a cruise from Tofino to Hot Springs Cove for a relaxing dip in the hot springs and a ramble in the rainforest. Try your hand at fishing for salmon by charter boat out of Ucluelet, or if scuba diving is your sport, there are guides there to acquaint you with the Barkley Sound area to explore.

10.3 TOFINO AIRPORT started as a World War II military base, part of the defense system for a vulnerable coastline. The 26 mile road from Tofino to Ucluelet, joining both ends of the Estowitsa peninsula, was rapidly completed during the war to connect the airbase with a seaplane base at Ucluelet. No attack came except for the submarine shelling of Estivan Point lighthouse up the coast. Today the base is the region's only commercial airfield.

200

An early print of a characteristic Nootka long house interior.

12.0 GRICE BAY ROAD: The bay is a broad placid estuary that serves as a feeding ground for a large waterfowl population. There is a picnic site on the shore and on the way there you will pass by the most westerly golf course in Canada. The Long Beach Golf Club is currently nine holes with plans to extend to 18 in time.

14.0 RADAR HILL: Site of a wartime radar installation, it is only a short drive up to this commanding viewpoint with a 360 degree panoramic view of the whole area. Take the time to drive up to the top and you will be well rewarded with an incredible vista of land and sea.

21.0 TOFINO is the end of the highway and jumping-off point for the central-Island coast. A small fishing port and service centre, Tofino's roots nevertheless reach into the earliest history of European contact with the British Columbia coast.

Neighbouring Clayoquot Indians, a clan of the Nootka, had many villages in the area. They trapped fish from the nearby rivers, gathered berries and food stocks from the forest, and erected cedar-planked longhouses for their people. They shared the great Nootka tradition of seeking the powerful whales out at sea, pursuing them in large open canoes, often beyond the sight of land. Surely a task for the bravest and ablest of the men.

The first fur traders into the area, the ambitious "Boston Traders" from the American east coast, began naming the prominent landmarks and met the famous Clayoquot leader, Chief Wickaninnish. Tofino itself was named by the Spanish, in honour of their famous hydrographer, Don Vincent Tofino, in 1792. Meares Island, offshore, was named by an early independent English trader and former Lieutenant under Captain Cook, John Meares, who precipitated the Nootka Incident that almost brought Spain and England to war. The site of historical Fort Defiance on Meares Island was the 1792 winter outpost for the intrepid American trader Captain Gray who later discovered and named the Columbia River.

Permanent European settlement in the area came with the first trading post on Stubbs Island in 1875; a store, church, and various scattered settlements dotted the offshore Islands until a new Anglican church at Tofino in 1913 provided a focus for the present townsite. This was followed by stores, a post office, fish camp, and logging camps with a sawmill. Previously, some optimistic farmers had opened up land on the peninsula.

Fishing has always been the main industry for Tofino. A small boatbuilding industry provided new boats for some local fishermen, and the government lifeboat was also stationed at the port to guard "those who go down to the sea in ships". For years the CPR's pocketliner "Princess Maquinna" was the only regular means of communication with the outside world. Its arrival every 10 days with mail, passengers, and freight was a major social event in the community. In 1940 the pressure of war brought an airplane landing field to Tofino, now still the area's only airport.

Remote from the mainstream of Island development, the Tofino area slowly developed in isolation, thriving on its roots in the sea and the forests. But today the new highway and National Park has opened new opportunities for the region and a new historical chapter for Tofino.

202

In the sheltered coves up the coast beyond Tofino, a visitor with a boat at his disposal can visit historic Ft. Defiance on Meares Island, Gibson Marine Park near the fishing village of Ahousat, or Maquinna Park at Hot Springs Cove.

WEST COAST MARITIME MUSEUM: Near the centre of Tofino is a private but ambitious collection of seafarer's memorabilia, including flotsam and jetsom from famous shipwrecks, old ship's logs and navigational instruments, and items from the eras of the fur-trade and colonial days. It's open seasonally, and well worth a visit.

A fishing crew raising the net after a "set".

Muchalat is typical of the many fjord-like inlets on the Island's west coast.

Campbell River to Gold River

THE Gold River road, like many Island highways, was once a limited industrial access road for the forest industry; its improvement and designation as a highway coincided with the new pulp mill and "instant town" at Gold River. Crossing through the panoramic mountain heartland of the Island, it is easily a route deserving the highest superlatives: here in its unassailable high mountain fortress perches the Golden Hinde, the Island's highest peak; here is its largest park, Strathcona, and one of its longest lakes, Buttle Lake. Here are the last of the Island's alpine glaciers, and here is Canada's highest waterfall, Della Falls. It is a region of dramatic and awesome proportions.

This paved highway travels through Strathcona Park and down the Heber River valley to Gold River and tidewater at Muchalat Inlet.

0.0 CAMPBELL RIVER TOURIST INFORMATION CENTRE: Proceed north on Highway 19. See maps 7, 8 and 9.

1.4 JUNCTION TO GOLD RIVER: Proceed on Highway 28. The road follows along the south bank of Campbell River for 2.8 miles.

2.4 QUINSAM CAMPGROUND: 31 campsites plus picnic grounds on the Quinsam River in Elk Falls Provincial Park. The river is 23 miles long and is considered one of the best steelhead rivers on the Island. Excellent fishing December to March.

3.0 **JOHN HART GENERATING STATION** is one-quarter mile from this junction. You can have a conducted tour through this hydro-electric plant, named for the late Honourable John Hart, Provincial Premier from 1941 to 1947.

4.1 **HISTORICAL POINT OF INTEREST:** The Campbell River fire of 1938 ravaged over 75,000 acres of prime forest and came within one and a half miles of Campbell River. The clouds of smoke darkened the sky so much that the lights in Courtenay had to be kept on most of the day. The smoke clouded the sky as far away as Portland, Oregon, 350 miles south. Soot fell on Vancouver, while over 1500 firefighters battled grimly for weeks to save timber and communities. Reforestation is evident as you travel through.

JUNCTION TO JOHN HART DAM: A short drive to the site. After crossing the dam, you will find a picnic site and a trail to a viewpoint overlooking Elk River Falls.

MORTON AND MOHUN LAKES are reached by crossing the dam and travelling for about another fourteen miles on gravel roads to the provincial campground at the lakes. There is a boat launching ramp, 24 campsites and 11 picnic sites. All of the lakes in this area are reputed to be excellent for fishing. See also the access from Highway 19 north of Campbell River on page 117.

6.0 **McIVOR LAKE:** A popular spot with a sandy beach, good swimming, picnicking, and paved boat ramp.

9.0 **ECHO LAKE:** Dolly Varden, Rainbow and Cutthroat trout can be caught all summer but April and October are the best months. Launching for trailer and car-top boats. Power boats are prohibited.

19.1 **STRATHCONA DAM:** One and a half miles from this junction is this earthfill dam, 170 feet high and 1800 feet wide, across the northern end of Upper Campbell Lake. The

206

reservoir is 30 miles long, providing storage for 620,000 acre-feet of water for the downstream generating station.

20.0 UPPER CAMPBELL LAKE is 15 miles long, one and a quarter miles wide. There is year round fishing for rainbow, cutthroat, and Dolly Varden, averaging 8 to 22 inches. Boats are available at Strathcona Lodge.

25.0 ELKHORN MOUNTAIN, elevation 7,190 feet, is the second highest mountain in the park, and can be seen to the west.

Campbell Lake with Elkhorn Mountain in the distance.

26.6 STRATHCONA PARK LODGE: While this lodge is still available to the traveller, its larger purpose is as the Strathcona Park Outdoor Education Centre, which offers to groups and individuals a base for education outside the classroom. The Centre stresses its commitment to assist in the development of environmental awareness in people.

30.7 JUNCTION: The Ralph River campground is 15 miles south down the east shore of Buttle Lake, where there are 73 campsites and a boat launching ramp. Another ramp will also be found one mile from this junction.

To continue on Highway 28 to Gold River, turn right and cross the original Campbell River channel as it leaves Buttle Lake on your left.

31.3 BUTTLE LAKE CAMPGROUND features 32 campsites on the northwest corner of the Lake.

BUTTLE LAKE was named for Commander John Buttle, a member of an official exploring party that discovered the lake in 1865. The lake is 23 miles long, one mile wide, and flows into Upper Campbell Lake. Commander Buttle's diary contains the following: "It (the lake) is surrounded by high mountains and its shores are bold and rocky. The only name I could get from the Indians for this lake was Conuma Ahhook, or in English, 'Mountain Lake', which I have adopted."

Rainbow and cutthroat trout up to six pounds, and Dollies up to twelve pounds, make for interesting lake fishing.

33.4 DOGWOOD: As you continue to Gold River along the west arm of Upper Campbell Lake, notice the profusion of dogwood trees (in full blossom from April to June) dotting the lower mountainsides. This is the floral emblem of the province.

37.0 BOAT LAUNCHING RAMP.

37.7 PARK BOUNDARY: You will be driving within Strathcona Provincial Park for approximately 10 miles.

STRATHCONA PROVINCIAL PARK: Whether proceeding on the Gold River road or taking a "side jaunt" down the eastern shore of Buttle Lake, you will shortly enter this, the oldest provincial park in British Columbia, named after Donald Alexander Smith, First Baron Strathcona and Mount Royal, a Canadian pioneer who drove the last spike linking Canada from Atlantic to Pacific by rail.

This half million acres of wilderness enclose the loftiest mountains on the Island. The peaks dominate the park scenery, with many summits perpetually under snow. Vancouver Island's highest point, the Golden Hinde (7,219 feet), rises almost at the centre of the park, several miles west of Buttle Lake. Countless

The great cascade of Della Falls.

lakes and tumbling rivers and creeks are found in lowlands and valleys where dense forests exist that were old when Captain James Cook landed in 1778 at Nootka Sound, a few miles from the park's western boundary.

DELLA FALLS, the highest waterfall in Canada and one of the highest in the world, with an overall drop of 1,443 feet, is located in the southern section of the park. It is accessible only to very experienced hikers by a 10-mile trail from the south end of Buttle Lake.

An excellent, comprehensive brochure with map published by the provincial Department of Recreation and Conservation is available at tourist information centres.

40.4 CERVUS CREEK AND LADY FALLS: A short walk can be taken to Lady Falls, on Cervus Creek, near its junction with the Elk River.

42.7 ELK RIVER CROSSING offers another excellent view of Elkhorn Mountain, with Kings Peak (6,774 feet) in the foreground.

45.5 DRUM LAKE and a number of smaller lakes in this area supply additional water by pipeline to the Upper Campbell Lake system.

47.0 STRATHCONA PARK WESTERN BOUNDARY: From approximately this point the watershed now flows west, and the highway descends roughly 1,000 feet to tidewater.

54.9 JUNCTION: Two miles to Antler Lake picnic site and seven miles to Muchalat Lake campground. The C.I.P. Company maintains 30 campsites and a boat ramp. Good trout fishing.

55.0 GOLD RIVER: Population 2,225. The town was incorporated in August 1965, under the "instant town" legislation passed the same year. It is a fully modern community, all-electric heat, underground wiring services, blacktopped streets, and modern shopping and service facilities. Peppercorn Park has

"Uchuck III", out of Gold River, serves remote spots on the west coast.

a natural setting of river and woods to make this a most pleasant and rewarding area to visit. A picnic site is located in the park.

62.4 TIDEWATER: Here the Gold River enters Muchalat Inlet; This is the site of the Canadian International Paper Company's modern pulp mill, constructed in 1965 to produce bleached kraft. Modern large ships enter Nootka Sound and cruise up the inlet to take the products of this mill to the markets of the world. Enquire about plant tours.

In addition to excellent salt water fishing in the Inlet, there are steelhead, rainbow and cutthroat trout in the Gold River.

A SCENIC CRUISE aboard the motor vessel "Uchuck III" is available Mondays and Wednesdays during July and August, to Friendly Cove in Nootka Sound. The seven-hour trip has both scenic and historical interest, as Friendly Cove is the place where Captain Cook and his men on H.M.S. Discovery were the first Europeans to set foot on Vancouver Island (1778) and began trading with the Nootka Indians. The sea otter furs Cook took away fetched such high prices in China, that soon a flourishing business was established by fur traders with the Indians under Chief Maquinna at their summer village at Friendly Cove. (See page 32).

THE FIRST VANCOUVER ISLAND SETTLERS: Chinese artisans and labourers were the first known strangers to settle on the Island. Brought from China in 1778 by the British Captain John Meares to build and maintain a base for his fur trading activities at Nootka, they also built the first schooner launched on the coast, the "North West America". As pawns in the "Nootka War", the Chinese labourers fell into Spanish hands. They tended the Spanish garrison and worked a small gold find at the head of Muchalet Inlet. Some reputedly took Indian wives; however, the eventual fate of this first band of settlers has not been determined.

The raising of a totem pole is a unique and solemn ceremony. This pole, raised at Alert Bay, is a memorial to the famous native carver Mungo Martin. Much of his work can be seen at the Provincial Museum in Victoria.

Highway 19 borders the Nimpkish River and Lake on its way north.

Mt. Cain can be seen from the road through the Nimpkish Valley.

213

Woss Community—home for loggers and their families in this rugged country.

The Cape Scott Trail from Holbert is the only way you can get to the wild and rugged 'top end' of the Vancouver Island, nearly 300 miles from Victoria.

Remains of the wagon found on the shore of Lake Cowichan.

The continuing clamour for an upgrading of the trail from Port Alberni to Cowichan Lake, (see page 189), to wagon road standards, resulted in the Government of the day finally letting a contract in the late 1890's to have the work done.

Legend would have it, that with only a part of the job done, the Contractor tired of it, advised the authorities that the job was completed and arranged a meeting at Cowichan Lake to collect his money.

He took his team and wagon down the completed section, took the wagon apart, loaded it on the backs of the horses and proceeded through the trail to the beginnings of the lake road, assembled his wagon and drove off to meet the Government man and collected his money. Leaving the wagon on the lake shore, he rode his horses back to Port Alberni.

The beaches of Vancouver Island offer innumerable possibilities for exploration and discovery.

Have Fun

YOU are invited in this chapter to do some beachcombing, dig for clams, perhaps explore a forest trail and acquaint yourself with the tall guardians of the Island's valleys and mountainsides. Eagles, cormorants, seals and whales—a great variety of wildlife may be caught by an observer with binoculars or camera. The many miles of coastline, encompassing almost as many different environments, are especially rich in opportunities for you to indulge in your favourite recreational pursuits, from ornithology to driftwood discovery. The parks and forests inland offer every kind of natural mood, and possibly a waterfall will refresh you during a lunch in the woods nearby.

ON THE BEACH

Any of the beaches and rocky headlands about the Island can keep you fascinated for a whole morning or afternoon. As the tides rise and fall, a continually changing scene is presented. The greatest range of seashore life is exposed when the tide is lowest. You might find a Japanese fishing float stranded among the driftwood, or overturn a rock to discover a dozen purple shore crabs scurrying deeper into the sand. With the aid of a strong magnifying glass you can study the myriad forms of colourful life in tide pools among the rocks.

Most veteran beachcombers take along a net bag to keep odds and ends in, wear sturdy sneakers (salt water will quickly

217

rot leather), and find a windbreaker desirable at any time of year. They respect the regulation against collecting on park beaches, and know that most marine creatures lose colour and acquire unpleasant odours if removed from their environment.

It is easy to become pre-occupied with what lies at your feet. Develop a habit of looking up frequently to stay aware of how far you're wandering from areas that will be dry when the tide returns. Many people have become dangerously isolated from the actual shore by fast-forming tidal channels.

The British Columbia Provincial Museum distributes at minimal cost an excellent series of handbooks covering every aspect of marine and seashore life.

Driftwood is so plentiful on the Island beaches that you can hike along it for miles without setting foot on the sand. If you find an interesting bit of wood, finishing it to a polish will demand a lot of work with successively finer grades of sandpaper. Don't be surprised if sand in the wood itself takes a toll on your favourite tools. A suggested finisher is shoe polish, or half a dozen polished coats of a solution of 5 parts beeswax shavings dissolved in 20 parts turpentine, and applied with a lint-free cloth.

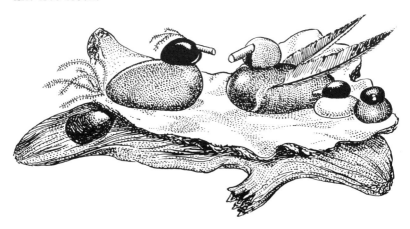

With some white glue and your imagination, you can construct both artistic and useful objects using any combination of shells, driftwood, wave-worn glass and stones, feathers, and so on.

Clam digging is anybody's sport on a good beach. As these molluscs vary in population, range, and edibility from season to season, it will be essential for you to obtain local information about conditions and legal limits. Two of the more popular clams found on the Island's shores are the butter clam, and the little neck clam ("rock cockle").

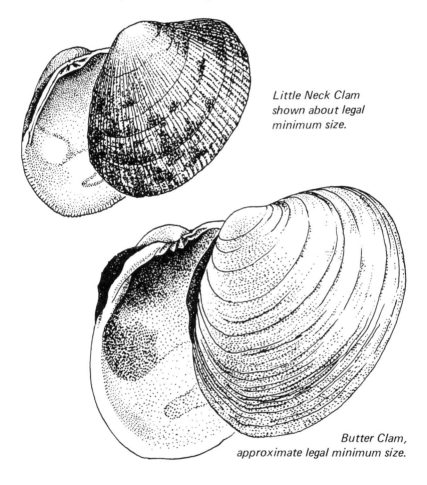

Little Neck Clam shown about legal minimum size.

Butter Clam, approximate legal minimum size.

For collecting you will need a bucket, a digging shovel, and some energy. Part of the fun is getting wet and dirty, so have extra clothes and hot beverages ready when you're done. The

219

lower the tide, the more clams you will find. They are indicated by squirts of water, small depressions in the sand, or by a surface bubble left where vibration has made the clam retreat downward. Dig rapidly about one foot, on the seaward side, lifting sand straight up, and reach in for the clam—they can burrow quickly.

Clams absorb sand and other material, and once opened their stomachs should be cut into and cleaned. Otherwise dig your clams about 12 hours before they are to be cooked, put them in a bucket of sea water in a cool shady place, add about a cup of oat- or cornmeal, and in this time they will sluice out their digestive systems.

Clam chowder for 4 people will require at least 4 quarts of clams in the shell, yielding about 2 cups of meat. Once the clams are steamed open, the juice should be saved and allowed to cool. Fry till crisp 2 or 3 slices of bacon and chop up. Fry till soft 1 small onion, chopped. Add 2 cups raw diced potatoes, 2 cups water, 1 tsp. salt, and a dash of pepper. Simmer until potatoes are cooked (about 10 minutes), then add the 2 cups of hot milk (not boiling). The clam nectar is prepared separately, thickening it by the addition of 2 tbsp. flour to cold juice, which you bring to a boil stirring constantly. Add 2 tbsp. butter and add the clam nectar to the chowder just before serving.

Pacific Oyster, often encrusted with barnacles and found attached to rocks.

Another popular feast will be yours if you scrub and rinse about 1 quart of clams (in shell) per person, then steam in a large covered pot with about a half cup of water for 4 quarts of clams until the shells start to open. Strain the accumulated broth through as fine a cloth as possible, remove a clam from its shell, dip into the broth, then into melted butter and enjoy.

The Pacific Oyster, especially between October and May, is a welcome "import" to Vancouver Island shores. Gatherers must obtain current local information about possible contamination areas. Oysters are found in "beds"—the best of course will be those exposed at the lowest tides. Commercial leases must be respected. Collect only intact oysters; they should close quickly when disturbed. To open a raw oyster is difficult—it's easier if you first place them in boiling water 3 minutes, drop into ice water, then insert a sturdy knife to cut the hinge muscle and run the blade between the shell halves, deeper half in your palm. Save and strain the juice for stew. Remove the oyster meat with a knife, and remove any shell fragments. The oysters can be put on a grill while in the shell if you simply want to eat them off the deeper half. Let them steam open but avoid overcooking. Sprinkle with lemon juice and savour your harvest.

Oyster stew is a good introduction to this seafood. For six people, melt ¼ cup of butter or margarine, add 1 pint of shucked oysters with their juice, and simmer till the meat is plump and ruffled along the edges (about 3 minutes). Add the oysters to 5 cups of hot milk with 1½ tsp. salt, some pepper, and other seasonings such as celery salt, Worchestershire sauce, paprika and serve.

IN THE WOODS

Whether taking a morning excursion into the forest, or a week-long journey into the mountains, the range of growth between diminutive starflower and mighty west coast trees presents you with profound contrasts. In the primeval settings you can taste berries and other foods that sustained the earliest human inhabitants of this region. The accompanying illustrations provide but a hint of the natural wealth around you.

Western Hemlock *(Tsuga heterophylla)*

*Short blunt needles
and small cones.*

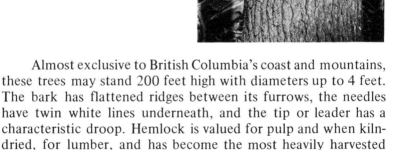

Bark on mature tree.

Almost exclusive to British Columbia's coast and mountains, these trees may stand 200 feet high with diameters up to 4 feet. The bark has flattened ridges between its furrows, the needles have twin white lines underneath, and the tip or leader has a characteristic droop. Hemlock is valued for pulp and when kiln-dried, for lumber, and has become the most heavily harvested species on the Island.

Douglas Fir *(Pseudotsuga menziessii)*

The largest native tree in Canada, this "fir" was named after David Douglas, a Scottish botanist who in the early 1800s explored much of the Pacific Northwest. Often 200 feet high and 3 to 6 feet in diameter, the trees are identified by the three-pronged bracts between the cone scales. Long the supreme commercial species, Douglas fir is renowned for its building and marine construction qualities of strength and hardness.

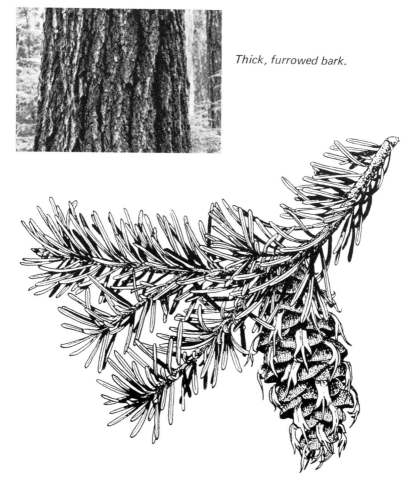

Thick, furrowed bark.

223

Western Red Cedar *(Thuja plicata)*

Small green cones become
woody when open.

Bark.

     Vancouver Island is home for these, the loftiest North American cedars. Many are 150 feet high with a trunk diameter of even 8 feet. Northwest coast Indians used these durable trees for sleek dug-out canoes, and wove mats and clothing from the thin strip-like bark. The spire taper of the trunk and the smooth, scaly and lacy leaves are easily recognized. The wood is marketed for shingles, siding, fenceposts, and interior uses.

224

Balsam Fir *(Abies amabilis)*

Combining the stature of coastal trees with the graceful, full form of alpine species, this fir is a pleasure to see in the coastal forest. It may grow 100 feet in height and have a diameter to 3 feet, and it has been brought out of the wild for ornamental purposes. The needles turn up and outward along the branches, and are not flattened as on grand fir. Balsam is a light wood, utilized for pulp and some construction.

Old bark. Smooth on younger trees.

Upright cones leave a spike when dried and dissipated in autumn.

For children the mystique of the woods encourages exploration—especially if hidden treasure is to be found. Put some chocolate bars or other treats in a plastic box or bag and hide them where natural landmarks, such as odd trees, rock outcrops, stumps, or your own stick-and-stone markers, can help indicate the secret location. Provide the treasure-hunters with a simple sketch map that includes essential clues.

From the absolute wilderness of the Cape Scott region's preserve, to the southernmost headlands and coves of East Sooke Park, the hiker can find in a grove of trees or the coolness of a stream the somber beauties that greeted the first explorers of Vancouver Island. The opportunities are endless, to rediscover silence and solitude, to develop a sense of independence, and to tap resources of strength and awareness you may have forgotten you had. With a pair of durable boots, lightweight backpacking equipment, and a selection of high-energy foods, you can find Edens of your own.

While you're in the woods, you become part of their ecologic community; almost anything you add or remove will affect, and perhaps damage, the balance of life. The challenge is to leave no trace of your having passed through. In some areas you have probably been dismayed to find trash at an otherwise idyllic campsite. People put it there, and only people can take it away—if you'll compact and bring out your refuse and a little of someone else's, that is genuine outdoorsmanship. When permitted, your fire should be made with small pieces of wood, to keep it controlled and the flames at low, practical proportions. The wise camper knows how easily his campfire can creep under humus and reappear in an old stump several yards from the coffeepot, long after the coffee's cold. Obviously, ashes must be soaked and spread with your hands, and if you scatter your cooking stones no one will know you were there. Best of all to use one of the fast efficient alcohol or gas cartridge stoves for cooking. These are light, compact, and save you searching for firewood.

Forest closures are occasionally in effect, when the summer has especially dry spells. Logging ceases and all access to the forests, whether for a hike or just berrypicking, may be unlawful until some raid reduces the "tinder box" conditions. Over the years, forest fires in British Columbia have ruined resources of inestimable recreational and utilitarian value and it takes years for the land to recover from devestation.

Current forest conditions are posted at ranger stations on the highways.

Public use of logging roads, which are maintained by the forest products companies, is neither safe or allowed during working hours, but most firms permit travel on the weekends and after hours. Flat tires may enrich your trip if you branch off, so remain on the main routes, and have a spare wheel, a shovel, and an axe or folding saw just in case. While "getting away from it all" in the wilder regions remember you're on your own. Have plenty of gas in the tank, extra food, a substantial first aid kit, and know in advance how you'll spend the night should you stray onto a long, dead-end branch road. Detailed maps are freely available at the various companies' regional offices during the work week. In a single recent year, one company alone admitted over 100,000 travellers on their roads. They camped, fished, hunted, and enjoyed the wilderness, but somehow left behind $80,000 damage through theft, vandalism, and fires—a poor thanks for the privilege of having access to the pleasures of the back country.

Logging trucks don't pull over for the vacationist.

CAMPING

The provincial Parks Branch maintains several fine campgrounds in some of the provincial parks. Each contains campsites featuring parking spur, tent space, table and fireplace. Many will accommodate small trailers or campers but no hook-up facilities are provided. The campgrounds generally have a small per night fee in effect from spring through early fall, and are gated between 11 p.m. and 7 a.m. There is no reservation system and occupancy is limited to fourteen days.

Some local regional boards, notably at the north end of the Island, have established camping areas, and many forest com-

228

panies have set aside attractive sites in remoter places. These various facilities are all good and well-used all summer. Numerous privately operated campgrounds, equally as interesting, provide further space. The fullest range of camping possibilities, such as in Strathcona Provincial Park and up-Island areas, are open to those who are equipped to be self-sufficient "off the beaten track."

TIPS FOR MOTHER
What to take—Cooking Equipment:

- ☐ Heavy cast iron frying pan.
- ☐ Pressure cooker, preferably heavy cast aluminum.
- ☐ Tea kettle or extra saucepan large enough to heat washing water.
- ☐ Dishpan and/or hand basin, of metal or enamel wear, for heating water.
- ☐ Large plastic tablecloth, usable as a waterproof covering overnight.
- ☐ Oven mitts are a good idea too.
- ☐ Pail for water.
- ☐ Although you may not wish to take your hibachi, the grills from it will be handy for toasting over the open fire. You can "cheat" a little by taking a bag of briquettes along for a good hot fire under your steaks.

What to take—clothing:

• If a dressed-up occasion is on your agenda, a separate suit-case containing the "city" clothes for the whole family is a fine idea, as it keeps these from being mixed about with the holiday garb in their individual cases or rucksacks.

• Have a large laundry bag on the go, so that as things become soiled they are immediately collected for the laundromat stop.

• Include spare runners for everyone in the family—they are great for wading in rough and rocky places. Don't forget, salt water is ruinous to leather.

• Light waterproof jackets with hoods should be kept handy against the chance of rain, or even the cool of evening and morning.

229

What to take—Food

● The new dried foods and instant beverages are a boon to the camper, not only saving time but also space and weight in food containers.

● Buying fresh fruit and vegetables along the way makes a pleasant change and will add to your interest and memory of the locality. Take advantage of fresh seafoods wherever possible. Almost every little town has a bake shop—try their breads and other goodies to add variety.

● If your children are the kind who stay in swimming until they're turning blue, try the old Scottish custom of giving them a "Shivering Bite"—any dry crackers to munch on, they'll love it. So pack some soda crackers, sea biscuits, grahams, or whatever in the beach basket.

● Take yourself to lunch every day by preparing it in advance. While all the supplies (butter, jam, cheese) are out for breakfast, make up the lunch sandwiches, fill the thermos with lunchtime drinks, and get the fruit and cookies out, too. For a change, boil up eggs in the water you are going to use at breakfast, and have hard-boiled eggs for lunch. Remember to put a container of salt in your lunch kit.

Entertainment

● If your job is a combination of navigator, cook, and program director you'll need a few tricks at hand to keep everyone happy and interested during the time on the road. Here are some games-on-the-go that may help:

● If you have a four- or five-year old who is learning his or her numbers, the child can be assigned to read the "Slow to 35"-type signs for the driver.

● Lucky number game: each member in the car picks a number from 0 to 9 as their number. As every car is passed the last number on the licence plate is noted, and the player whose number it is gets a tick on his score. For example, if the passing motorist has number ABF 514, the player who has chosen "4" gets the point. At day's end, or the period designated, the winner, with the most numbers, gets the prize or the choice of the next activity.

● If your family are a bit older, another licence plate game involves "collecting" the names of all the provinces and states.

Some Forest Foods

Shown are but a few common plants: **Western Swordfern** (1) has hilt-like prong on each leaflet or pinna, and rootstock can be roasted; **Salmonberry** (2) features pink flowers and edible orange fruit; **Salal** (3) yields tasty purple berries; **Red Huckleberry** (4), very edible, has green stems; the blue berries of **Oregon Grape** (5) make fine jelly; young unfolding stems of **Western Bracken** (6) resemble asparagus when cleaned and boiled; trailing **Blackberry** (7) is delicious raw or in pies, or ice cream flavouring.

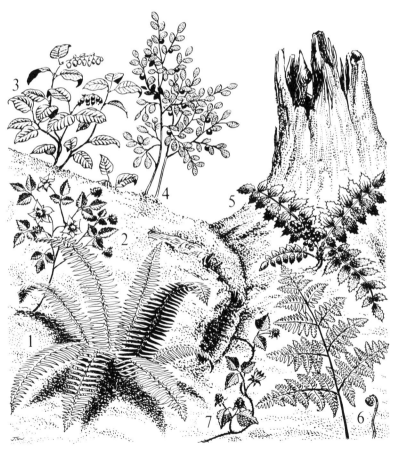

A forestry company helps you to identify some of the wild flowers to be found in an area they have set aside. See page 180.

It will be surprising how many different names you'll see.

• Plan to make frequent stops for everyone, particularly the driver, to stretch and do this where you can take a walk in the woods and enjoy the wildflowers and trees. Take an interest in identifying them and observing things like moss on the northern side of trees, measuring the circumference of trees by handspans, and so on.

• If you're having your lunch in the woods, see how well you and the children can disguise your presence, upon leaving, so no one would guess you'd been there.

• Do be prepared for a "rainy day" with decks of cards, checkers or chess, monopoly, or any other favourite games, toys (just a couple), as well as books. Take the chance to get acquainted with the Milestones ahead of you.

• Let everyone participate in the travelling by using lots of maps, guidebooks, travel books, and any local brochures available.

• Lastly, and most important, bring along binoculars, camera, compass, musical instruments perhaps, and for young artists sketching pads, pencils, paints, and crayons. Every good trip deserves to be recorded: designate someone to maintain a journal, or assign this on a rotating basis. Or how about putting the day's highlights on a cassette tape recorder, to be played back with the home movies or slides?

Happy adventuring to everyone, especially Mother.

WILDFLOWERS

The Island's famous scenery is greatly enhanced by the outstanding variety of flora to be found. From sea level to alpine meadows, wildflowers particularly, will make their contribution to your enjoyment of the outdoors.

Parks are, of course, the prime conservancy areas. An example is Thetis Lake Park near Victoria where over 300 species of flowering plants have been found, but, wherever you go, an abundance of seasonal wildflowers will be there for you to discover. The photograph on the preceding page shows how one forestry company helps you to identify some of the species to be found in an area they have set aside. See page 180.

Certainly, a valuable companion would be "Trees, Shrubs and Flowers to know in British Columbia" by Chess Lyons.

ROCKHOUNDING

On an island so varied in its geologic structure, anyone searching for beautiful stones will find a kaleidoscope of specimens. Collecting is easiest where gravel beds are found free of dense vegetation. Most gravel bars along the Island's coast were deposited by massive glaciers that once scoured the valleys, carrying boulders, till, and gravels out to the seashore. Creek and stream outlets continue to issue the greatest variety of stones. Some larger rocks yield symmetric patterns or interesting crystal formations when sliced open, and smaller smoothed agates and pebbles can make a colourful collection for a child, or perhaps be used for your own hand-made jewelry.

An important word about relics and archaeological materials—any disturbance of such items or their locations may shortchange the record of ages past, and digging or removal result in stiff penalties unless a special permit has been granted. The Archaeological Sites and Advisory Board appreciates the cooperation of the public in protecting these priceless areas.

GOLFING

Nestled in amongst farms in quiet valleys, or skirting wind-swept shorelines, Island golf courses have magnificent settings that always invite return matches, whatever your handicap. Greater Victoria has nine golf courses and additional courses are found at Sooke, Duncan, Chemainus, Nanaimo, Qualicum, Alberni, Courtenay, Comox, Campbell River, and on Saltspring, Galiano, and Pender Islands. At Port Alice, near the Island's rugged northern coast, are Canada's most westerly fairways.

TRAIN RIDE ANYONE?

The E. & N. Railway runs a round trip passenger service up-Island to Courtenay daily, except Sunday. Leaving Victoria at 8:15 a.m. from the Victoria terminal, and returning at 5:40 p.m., this is an easy way for the family to appreciate the overall scenery of the Island's eastern coastline. There are no refreshments aboard, and with limited stops along the way, it is wise to take along an old-fashioned "shoe-box" lunch of enough goodies and beverages for the day.

FISHING

Before you seek out that handsome rainbow or cutthroat, in non-tidal waters you'll need a fishing license if you are a non-resident of Canada or a resident 18 years of age or older. Licenses and the Summary of Sport Fishing Regulations are available at sport shops and tourist information centres. In tidal waters, either resident or non-resident is required to have a personal license, but non-residents bringing a boat into the country for fishing must have it licensed. Salt water fishing information as well is readily found at fishery offices and the outlets mentioned above.

MARINE PARKS

Relax with an iced tea in a sun-dappled cove, straddle a buoyant driftwood log and paddle a ways along the beach—there are a whole raftload of things to do at the provincial marine parks. About a dozen of these are in close proximity to Vancouver Island and are representative of the unique charm that has made the Strait of Georgia environs a yachtsman's paradise.

Well aware of the recreational potential in these waters, the provincial Parks Branch, since 1957, has been establishing this series' of parks. Most have safe anchorages and/or floats, some have camping and picnic areas, drinking water at some, and all include refuse disposal and sanitary facilities. These features have been designed to be in accord with the natural state of each park.

You'll find many signs that this animal has passed by—the one creature not especially protected in parks. Suggestions on how to control this pest will be welcomed.

Litterbug droppings.

235

HAVING A DRINK

For a cool Chablis with a fresh caught salmon, or a tall beer on a hot day, a visitor will have to turn to the Island's only liquor outlets—the provincial government liquor stores. These are found in most communities, operating during the usual store hours.

Draft and bottled beer and cider is sold in hotel "beer parlours", beers, wines, ciders, liqueurs and spirits in "licensed" lounges and "licensed" restaurants. Hence the meaning of the sign "licensed" that you will see from time to time. Drinkers must be nineteen years of age or older to indulge in their "aqua vitae."

British Columbia wines are competitive with imports, at least in price, and the province is developing a commendable wine industry.

WEATHER

Almost anywhere you go on the Island, you'll find the sea influencing the weather. In summer, cool off-shore breezes moderate the sun's warmth, and in the winter months of December through March coastal regions rarely receive more than a few occasional inches of snow. During late fall to early spring, most Island residents are never too far from their rainwear, and wool garments are favoured against the autumn mornings, the damp air of winter and the occasional cool summer evening. Some of the finest weather occurs during April to September and October, when the skies are brilliantly clear and the air crisp. At any time of year, have something to wear to break the ever-present ocean breezes.

FERRIES

The ferries are a delightful and exciting introduction to Vancouver Island. The voyage allows you time for reading up about what to do, to enjoy a relaxing meal in the dining room, and to stroll along the decks. Hosts of sharp-eyed gulls ride the ship's slipstream, watching for cast-off galley scraps, and many

236

craft from ocean-going freighters to sailing yachts can be seen plying the various channels. The whole venture is a refreshing change of pace, for the driver especially. And as the mainland slides away astern, you sense a thrill in anticipation of what new experiences the mountainous island looming ahead may offer.

The different ferry routes and their respective terminal points are listed below, and are shown on the map on pages 16 and 17. The sailing schedules vary from season to season, so check by telephone while making plans.

Mainland Terminal	Island Terminal	Carrier Company	Crossing Time
Prince Rupert	Port Hardy	B.C. Ferry*	18 hours
Powell River	Comox	B.C. Ferry	1:30 hrs.
Horseshoe Bay	Nanaimo	B.C. Ferry	1:35 hrs.
Tsawwassen	Swartz Bay	B.C. Ferry	1:30 hrs.
Anacortes, Wash.	Sidney	Wash. State	3:00 hrs.
Seattle, Wash.	Victoria	B.C. Steamships**	4:15 hrs.
Port Angeles, Wash.	Victoria	Black Ball	1:35 hrs.

*Vehicle reservations required.

**Summer months only.

COMMERCIAL SERVICES

From the internationally known Empress Hotel in Victoria, to cosy, rustic cottages at out-of-the-way lakeside resorts, private enterprise on Vancouver Island has made every kind and quality of accommodation available. From intriguing handcraft shops to complete department stores, automobile service centers, and excellent restaurants, all imaginable goods and services contribute in great measure to the Island's reputation for hospitality, Be assured that your every need can be cared for.

TOURING AIDS

The Provincial Department of Travel Industry at Victoria, publishes yearly an impressive amount of information about recreation and travel throughout the province. Most helpful is the comprehensive and well detailed Annual Tourist Directory and the Provincial Road Map. These are obtainable free by written request or by personal call at the department's office at 1117 Wharf Street, Victoria, or the many tourist information centres on the Island. This well-organized material will assist you considerably to enjoy your visit. The Directory is particularly useful for it goes far beyond accommodation information with details on customs and immigration, auto insurance suggestions, firearms, currency exchange, pets and much more.

RADIO STATIONS

Numerous island stations keep travellers informed about road conditions, special holiday events, along with local weather analysis and general news. Their frequencies are as follows:

Alert Bay	CBRY- 1340	Port Alberni	CJAV - 1240
	FM - 105.1		FM - 98.1
Campbell River	CFWB- 1490	Port Alice	CBUX- 1170
	CBYT-FM- 104.5	Port Hardy	CBRW- 630
Coal Harbour	CBKO- 540		CFNI - 1240
Courtenay	CFCP - 1440	Sayward	CBKU- 630
Duncan	CKAY - 1500	Tahsis	CBXP - 1240
Gold River	CBKJ - 740	Ucluelet	CBXQ- 540
Nanaimo	CHUB- 1570	Woss	CBTW-FM - 92.9
	CKEG- 1350	Victoria	CFAX - 1070
	CKGS - 1260		CJVI - 900
Parksville	CHPQ - 1370		CKDA- 1220
			CFMS-FM- 98.5

SAYING IT RIGHT

Many Vancouver Island and northwest coast names derive from the Spanish and British explorations of this region. Few of these pose pronunciation difficulties, but the extensive use of distinctive Indian words presents most visitors with some tongue twisters. These refer to Coast Salish, Nootka, or Kwakiutl territorial names applied by the members of these tribes who at some time have occupied a specific portion of the coastal or inland areas. The following guide offers you help in expressing the more frequently encountered names:

238

Caycuse	KY-cue-s
Esquimalt	ess-KWY-malt
Euclataw	YOU-clawtaw
Juan de Fuca	WAHN-duh-FEW-kah
Koksilah	koke-SIGH-lah
Kwakiutl	kwaw-KYOU-tl
Kwasksista	kwawask-SISS-tah
Kyuquot	KEOH-kwaht
Muchalat	MUCK-ah-laht
Nanaimo	nah-NIGH-mo
Qualicum	KWAHLI-kuhm
Saanich	SAN-nitch
Salish	SAY-lish
Sooke	SOOK
Tofino	tow-FEEN-o
Tsartlip	SART-lip
Tsawwassen	saw-WAH-sen
Tzouhalem	zoo-HAY-lehm
Ucluelet	you-CLEW-leht
Youbou	YOU-bo

RECOMMENDED READING

It is not practical to list all the good books that would contribute to your knowledge and enjoyment of Vancouver Island. There are many to satisfy many diverse interests. Here are just a few:

- Trees, Shrubs and Flowers to know in British Columbia, by C.P. Lyons.

- The West Coast Trail, by the Sierra Club.

- Logging Road Travel, by Alec Merriman.

- Outdoors With Alec Merriman, (Fishing).

- Breakers Ahead, by R. Bruce Scott, (West Coast Shipwrecks).

- Bicycling Vancouver Island and the Gulf Islands, by S. Priest.

- The Gulf Islands, by Bruce Obee.

- Vancouver Island Ghost Towns, by T.W. Patterson.
- Key to Victoria, available at hotels and the Tourist Burea.
- Victoria On Foot, walking tours of Victoria's Old Town.
- Victoria in a Knapsack, by the Sierra Club.
- Hiking Trails of Victoria and Southern Vancouver Island, by the Outdoor Club of Victoria.
- The Naturalist's Guide to the Victoria Region, edited with contributions by Jim Weston and David Sterling.
- Home Port: Victoria, a maritime history by Ursula Jupp.
- Trackside, points of interest along the E.&N. Railway.
- Boss Whistle, a history of Island Coal Mining by Lynne Bowen.
- Vancouver Island's West Coast, a history by George Nicholson.
- Vancouver Island Fishin' Holes, by Mike Crammond.
- Tourist Map of Vancouver Island, by Informap. "Recommended"
- Touring Map & Directory of British Columbia, by Informap.
- Map: Provincial Parks of Vancouver Island.
- Island Pubbing, by Bob Tyrrell and Boyd Corrigan.

A Parting Thought . . .

Vancouver Island is more than just a unique place to visit. It is a way of life that provides opportunities for the unhurried visitor to experience a refreshment of the soul. This special charm of this special place is the natural heritage of all.

> *"A good man leaves an inheritance*
> *for his children's children."*
> *Proverbs 13:22*

MAP **1**

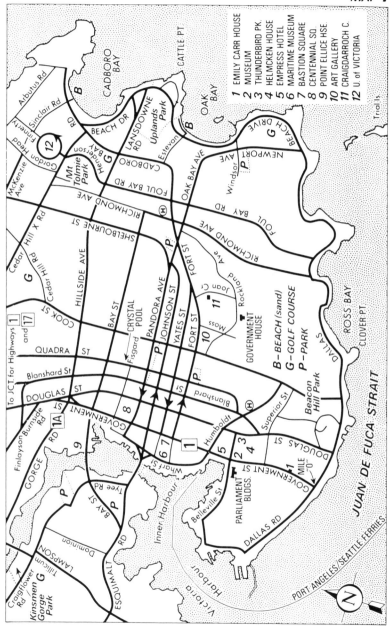

1 EMILY CARR HOUSE
2 MUSEUM
3 THUNDERBIRD PK.
4 HELMCKEN HOUSE
5 EMPRESS HOTEL
6 MARITIME MUSEUM
7 BASTION SQUARE
8 CENTENNIAL SQ
9 POINT ELLICE HSE
10 ART GALLERY
11 CRAIGDARROCH C.
12 U. of VICTORIA

B – BEACH (sand)
G – GOLF COURSE
P – PARK

MAP *2*

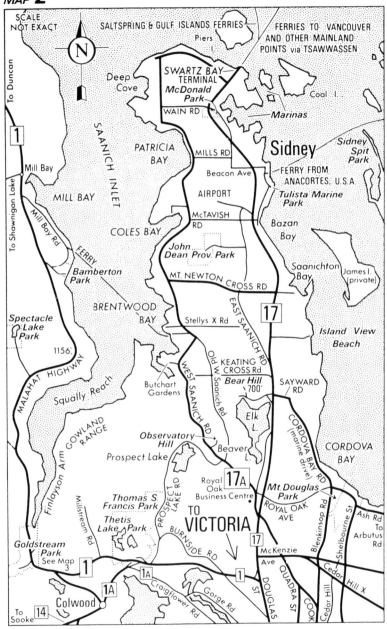

SCALE
NOT EXACT

SALTSPRING & GULF ISLANDS FERRIES

Piers I.

FERRIES TO VANCOUVER
AND OTHER MAINLAND
POINTS via TSAWWASSEN

To Duncan

N

Deep
Cove

SWARTZ BAY
TERMINAL

*McDonald
Park*

WAIN RD.

Marinas

Coal I.

SAANICH INLET

PATRICIA
BAY

MILLS RD.

Sidney

*Sidney
Spit
Park*

1

Mill Bay

MILL BAY

Beacon Ave

AIRPORT

FERRY FROM
ANACORTES, U.S.A.

*Tulista Marine
Park*

To Shawnigan Lake

Mill Bay Rd.

COLES BAY

McTAVISH
RD.

*John
Dean Prov. Park*

Bazan
Bay

FERRY

*Bamberton
Park*

MT. NEWTON CROSS RD.

Saanichton
Bay

James I.
(private)

*Spectacle
Lake
Park*

1156'

BRENTWOOD
BAY

Stellys X Rd.

EAST SAANICH RD.

17

*Island View
Beach*

MALAHAT HIGHWAY

Squally Reach

Butchart
Gardens

WEST SAANICH RD.

Old W. Saanich Rd.

KEATING
CROSS Rd.

*Bear Hill
700'*

SAYWARD
RD.

GOWLAND RANGE

Finlayson Arm

*Observatory
Hill*

Prospect Lake

*Elk
L.*

Beaver
L.

CORDOVA BAY RD.
(marine drive)

**CORDOVA
BAY**

Millstream Rd.

*Thomas S.
Francis Park*

PROSPECT LAKE RD.

Royal
Oak
Business Centre

17A

*Mt. Douglas
Park*

ROYAL OAK
AVE.

Blenkinsop Rd.

Shelbourne St

Ash Rd.
To
Arbutus
Rd

*Goldstream
Park*
See Map
3

*Thetis
Lake Park*

TO
VICTORIA

17

McKenzie
Ave.

Cedar Hill

Cedar Hill X

1

1A

BURNSIDE RD.

DOUGLAS ST

QUADRA ST.

COOK

1A

Craigflower Rd.

Gorge Rd.

ST.

1

14

To
Sooke

Colwood

MAP **3**

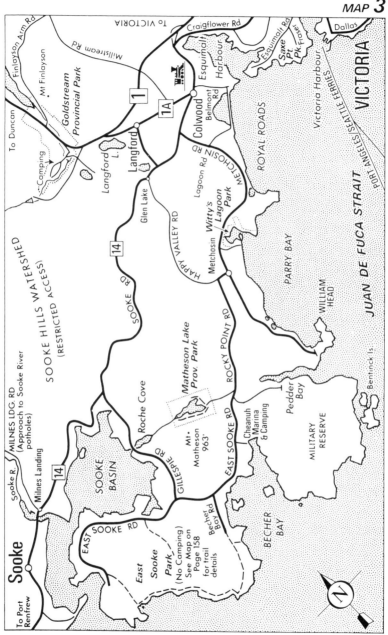

MAP **4**

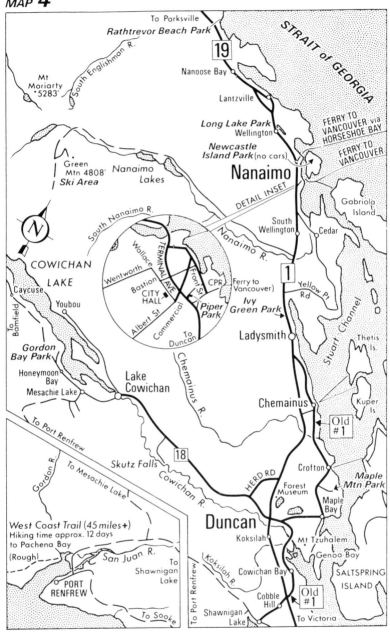

MAP **5**

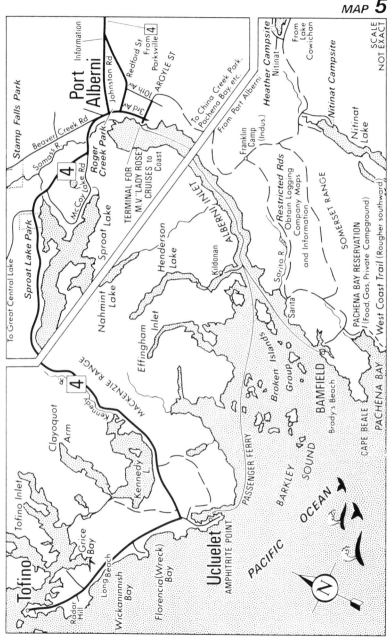

SCALE
NOT EXACT

From
Lake
Cowichan

Heather Campsite
Nitinat

Nitinat Campsite

Franklin
Camp
(Indus.)

*Nitinat
Lake*

Restricted Rds
Obtain Logging
Company Maps
and Information

SOMERSET RANGE

Sarita R.

Sarita

PACHENA BAY RESERVATION
(Food, Gas, Private Campground)

West Coast Trail (Rougher southward)

PACHENA BAY

CAPE BEALE

Brady's Beach

BAMFIELD

Broken Islands Group

BARKLEY SOUND

PASSENGER FERRY

Kildonan

ALBERNI INLET

Henderson
Lake

Effingham
Inlet

Nahmint
Lake

Sproat Lake

Roger
Creek Park

TERMINAL FOR
M.V. "LADY ROSE"
CRUISES to
Coast

To China Creek Park,
Pachena Bay, etc.

From Port Alberni

Information

Redford St
From
PARKSVILLE
ARGYLE ST

10th Av.

3rd Av.

Johnston Rd

Port
Alberni

Beaver Creek Rd

Somass R.

Stamp Falls Park

McCoy Lake Rd

Sproat Lake Park

To Great Central Lake

MACKENZIE RANGE

Kennedy R.

Clayoquot
Arm

Kennedy L.

Tofino Inlet

Grice
Bay

Long Beach

Radar
Hill

Wickanninish
Bay

Florencia (Wreck)
Bay

Ucluelet
AMPHITRITE POINT

PACIFIC OCEAN

Tofino

245

MAP 6

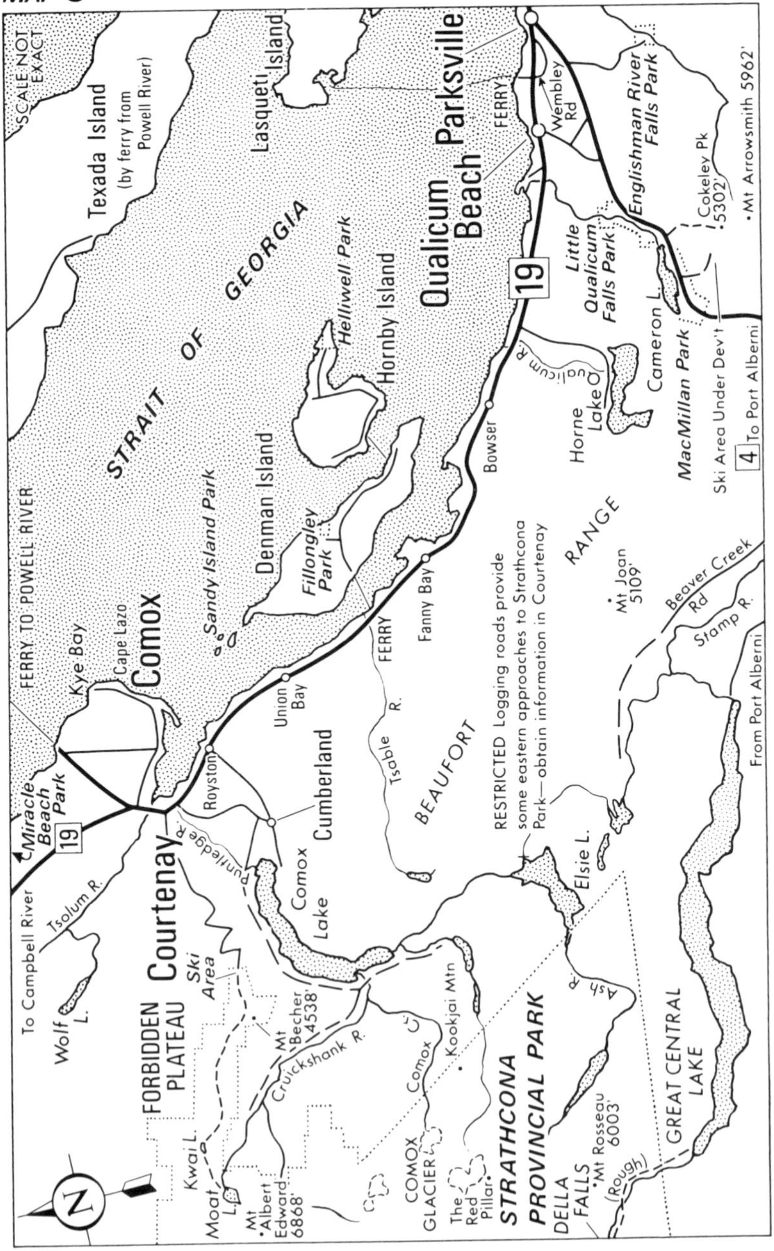

SCALE NOT EXACT
Texada Island
(by ferry from Powell River)
Lasqueti Island
Parksville
Qualicum Beach
FERRY
Wembley Rd
Englishman River Falls Park
Cokeley Pk 5302'
Mt Arrowsmith 5962'
STRAIT OF GEORGIA
Helliwell Park
Hornby Island
19
Little Qualicum Falls Park
Cameron L.
MacMillan Park
Ski Area Under Dev't
4 To Port Alberni
Qualicum R.
Horne Lake
Bowser
Denman Island
Sandy Island Park
Fillongley Park
Fanny Bay
FERRY TO POWELL RIVER
Comox
Cape Lazo
Kye Bay
Union Bay
RANGE
Mt Joan 5109'
Beaver Creek Rd
Stamp R.
From Port Alberni
RESTRICTED Logging roads provide some eastern approaches to Strathcona Park—obtain information in Courtenay
BEAUFORT
Tsable R.
Miracle Beach Park
Royston
Cumberland
Courtenay
Puntledge R.
Comox Lake
Elsie L.
To Campbell River
Tsolum R.
Wolf L.
FORBIDDEN PLATEAU
Ski Area
Mt Becher 4538'
Cruickshank R.
Comox Cr.
Kookjai Mtn
Ash R.
STRATHCONA PROVINCIAL PARK
GREAT CENTRAL LAKE
Kwai L.
Moat L.
Mt Albert Edward 6868'
COMOX GLACIER
The Red Pillar
DELLA FALLS
Mt Rosseau 6003'
(Rough)
N

MAP 7

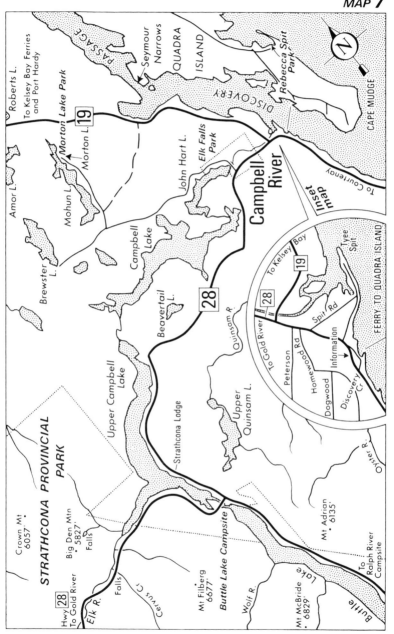

MAP **8**

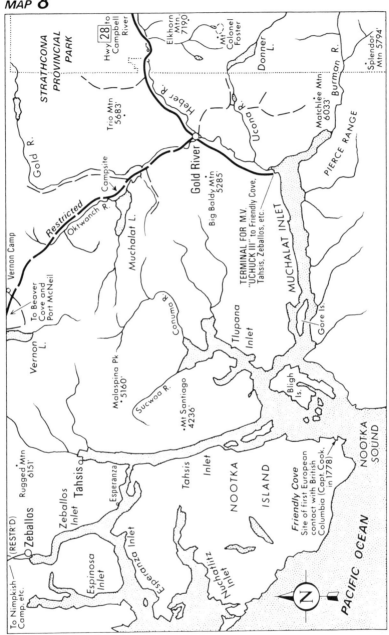

STRATHCONA PROVINCIAL PARK

Hwy 28 to Campbell River

Elkhorn Mtn. 7190'

Mt. Colonel Foster

Donner L.

Splendor Mtn 5794'

Gold R.

Trio Mtn 5683'

Heber R.

Ucona R.

Matchlee Mtn 6033'

Burman R.

PIERCE RANGE

Campsite

Restricted

Oktwanch R.

Gold River

Big Baldy Mtn 5285'

Muchalat L.

Vernon Camp

To Beaver Cove and Port McNeil

Vernon L.

Conuma R.

Malaspina Pk 5160'

Sucwoa R.

Mt Santiago 4236'

Tlupana Inlet

TERMINAL FOR MV. "UCHUCK III" to Friendly Cove, Tahsis, Zeballos, etc.

MUCHALAT INLET

Gore Is.

Bligh Is.

Friendly Cove
Site of first European contact with British Columbia (Capt. Cook, in 1778)

NOOTKA SOUND

NOOTKA ISLAND

Tahsis Inlet

Esperanza

Tahsis

Zeballos Inlet

Rugged Mtn 6151'

(RESTR'D)

Zeballos

To Nimpkish Camp, etc.

Espinosa Inlet

Esperanza Inlet

Nuchatlitz Inlet

PACIFIC OCEAN

N

248

MAP 9

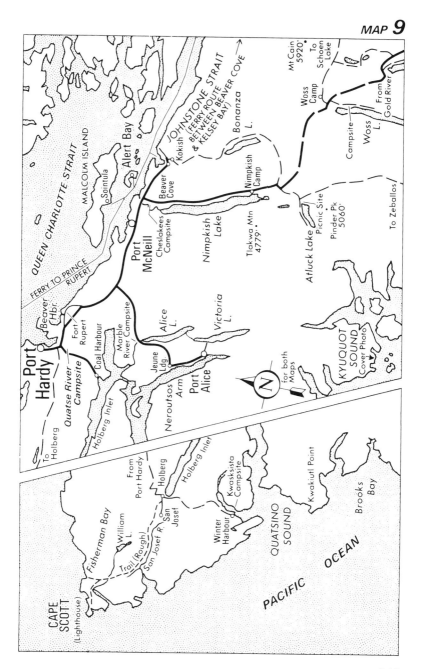

Index

251

252

PICTURE CREDITS

British Columbia Government:
Front and back cover and pages
13 . 18 . 29 . 31 . 32 . 52 . 58 . 60 .
61 . 70 . 72 . 90 . 91 . 100 . 110 .
130 . 138 . 139 . 142 . 148 . 150 .
155 . 194 . 196 . 203 . 204 . 209 .
216. 228. 191. 10. 212. 213.
214.

Laura Griffin: 11

Murray Galbraith: 68 .

Eric Pattison: 68 .

Du Pont of Canada: 116 .

Butchart Gardens: 132 .

Fred Corfield: 169 . 172 .

Parks Canada: 199 .

George McCandless: 211 .

The Victorian Weekly: 197

Upper Islander: 117

George Butler: 98

Cathy Pattison: 149

British Columbia Archives: 2 . 3 .
38 . 39 . 40 . 42 . 46 . 49 . 56 . 62 .
76 . 78 . 85 . 88 . 90 . 104 . 108 .
146 . 166 . 176 . 184 . 201 .

British Columbia Dept. of Forestry:
24 . 120 . 163 . 214 . 222 . 223 .
224 . 225 . 227 .

Steve Cannings: 9 .

Bob Russell: 27 . 183 .

Chess Lyons: 37 . 81 . 102 . 105 .
161 . 175 .

Jim Weston/Comfort Company:
14 . 72 . 109 .

Dave Chauvin/Comfort Company:
186 .

Alberni Valley Times: 193 .

K. Pattison: 71, 127. 207.
213. 232. 72. 8. 9. 215.

Kind permission was given by George Clutesi to use the stanza on page 2.
It is from the poem "West Coast Indian" which appears in full in his book
"Son Of Raven Son Of Deer", published by Gray's of Sidney, B.C.

Captain Vancouver's comments on page 3 are from his journal, "A Voyage
Of Discovery", May 1792.

Notes

Notes